Decorating with Paper

Decorating with Paper

CREATIVE LOOKS WITH WALLPAPERS, ART PRINTS, GIFT WRAP, AND MORE

DONNA LANG AND LUCRETIA ROBERTSON

PHOTOGRAPHY BY DENNIS KRUKOWSKI
FLOWERS BY DAVID MADISON OF DMHD

CLARKSON POTTER/PUBLISHERS
NEW YORK

Photographs on pages 149, 157 and 163 are reprinted with the permission of Simplicity Pattern Co. Inc.

Published by Clarkson Potter, Inc., 201 East 50th Street, New York, New York 10022. Member of the Crown Publishing Group.

Random House, Inc. New York, Toronto, London, Sydney, Auckland

CLARKSON N. POTTER, POTTER and colophon are trademarks of Clarkson N. Potter, Inc.

Manufactured in Hong Kong

Design by Karen Lee Grant and Andrzej Janerka

Library of Congress Cataloging-in-Publication Data

Lang, Donna.
   Decorating with paper : Creative looks with wallpapers, art prints, gift wrap, and more / by Donna Lang and Lucretia Robertson; photography by Dennis Krukowski; flowers by David Madison.
      p.   cm.
   Includes index.
   1. Wallpaper.   2. Decorative paper.   3. Interior decoration.   I. Robertson, Lucretia.   II. Title.
NK3395.L36   1993
747′.9—dc20   92-30331
                                                 CIP

ISBN 0-517-57753-4 (cloth)
ISBN 0-517-88124-1 (paper)

10 9 8 7 6 5 4 3 2 1

First Edition

For Lucretia Speziale Robertson   1944–1992

To everything she undertook, Lucretia brought vision,

creativity, energy, intelligence (and sometimes controversy)—always

making her world and the worlds of those

she touched more beautiful.

—D. L.

Contents

Foreword

The art of découpage was a first love of mine.

As a child, I was fascinated by paper cutouts, and as a young mother, I thrilled to see my girls, Apple and D.B., captured by the idea that this was fun to do.

Both my daughters and later my granddaughter, Susan, caught on quickly. Today, Apple (Mrs. Parish Bartlett) produces both découpage and décollage works for her shop, La Ruche, in Boston. D.B. (Mrs. Riley Gilbert) is an accomplished artist, producing the most intricate patterns on both tin boxes and hurricane glasses for lamps. Their work far surpasses mine in its sophistication, refinement, and detail, but I still love to collect the pictures that form the visions of découpage in my mind.

I am delighted by the numbers of people who have been inspired by my work and by the technique itself. At its best, découpage brings to the house a sense of humor, lightheartedness, and simplicity that refreshes.

MRS. HENRY PARISH II

This memorabilia tabletop was made by découpage artist Diane Denning Miller of Parish Hadley Associates to commemorate Mrs. Parish's eightieth birthday.

Preface

"In Charleston, West Virginia, the summers were long and hot and even going to Winston-Salem, North Carolina, to my grandmother's farm, couldn't take my mind off the heat. But for me, the quickest way to escape anyplace I found too hot or too boring or too noisy or too anything at all was to play with my paper dolls. The dolls could fly to Paris, wear their fancy clothes, carry their hatboxes, meet exciting people. I would sit out under the old elm behind the house, lovingly turning the pages in the books of beautiful clothes, carefully choosing which I would cut out and add to the ever-growing collection I kept organized in shoeboxes in my room. By the time I was eight, I had finally perfected the art of customizing Marilyn Monroe's right-facing wardrobe to fit Jane Powell's left-facing figure. Working with my mother's manicuring scissors, I swiveled the little dresses and suits around and around on their shiny tips, clipping and trimming, patiently working around the hat feather, the lace petticoat, and the poodle on a leash, until I could perfectly fit the fashion to the figure."

Now, more years down the road than either of us cares to ponder, I often watch Donna sitting in a quiet corner on a busy job site, surrounded with clutter, workmen, and noise, working silently with the client's chosen papers, cutting fearlessly into costly all-over prints to create small details or borders, tirelessly trimming into the pattern along the bottom edges of ready-made borders and completely changing their personalities. I am reminded of the little girl for whom printed paper was the beginning, not the end, of the fun.

We have always been fascinated by paper—Donna with her dolls and scrapbooks, and I with unusual bits and pieces used as drawing and calligraphy papers. As we grew and began professional careers, first in fashion and later in interior design, papers provided the little something extra in the preparation of reports and presentations, and ultimately became an important element in our interior design projects. And, since decorating creatively with a wide variety of papers offers a bounty of artistic and decorative possibilities without daunting technical restraints, we have written this book, hoping to challenge and inspire you to roll up your sleeves, pull out a pot of paste and your favorite scissors, and create beautiful "paperworks" of your own.

LUCRETIA ROBERTSON
DONNA LANG

Introduction

Even though we had formalized our professional partnership nearly a month earlier, Lang/Robertson, Ltd., *really* began in March of 1975 in a dusty third-floor room of a designer showhouse. Excitedly digging into our handbags, we each produced the one swatch we had culled from the vast New York design marketplace . . . the one we were prepared to fight for, convinced it would be perfect for this project, our first as a team. It was the same swatch.

To this day, we smile when we remember the surprise of seeing those two identical pieces of bright red fabric. We had known each other for years, had worked for the same companies, greeted each other in the halls, attended the same meetings. But we didn't really know each other until

that morning. There have been many similar incidents over the years, all of them reaffirming the compatibility of this partnership. In fact, in the beginning, the only thing we couldn't get together on was wallpaper. Donna loved it. I thought papering was the easy way out. The truth of the matter was that I knew very little about paper. We had come into this partnership with long experience working with fabric, and once you've lived with upholstered walls, papering can seem like an also-ran. It was, on my part, discrimination based on ignorance, and it was soon to change.

Over the years, my fascination with the versatility and the beauty of printed papers has grown to the point of obsession. Lang/Robertson's corporate design files, once filled to the

brim with little pieces of fabric, now run A to Z with folders stuffed with hundreds of neatly arranged, carefully folded wallpapers and borders. Donna, being the more adventurous of the two of us, has routinely knocked my socks off with combinations of papers and borders that, on the design table, defy association. How could she put that . . . with THAT! But she does, and in her own quiet way makes a brilliant and magical change in the room.

Not only do we put wallpapers and borders into our files, keeping them, if they are particularly well designed or beautifully colored, even after they have been discarded from the supplier's collection; we collect other, less expected papers as well. Our art paper drawers hold wide ranges of painted papers from Pantone and Color Aid; unusual handmades from all over the world; rice papers with fibers, Japanese papers with little leaves or twigs or specks of other materials pressed in; Italian calligraphy papers and parchments; glorious marble papers.

Even humble materials such as packaging papers make our collection: several weights of kraft paper, corrugated cardboard, and a group of little torn squares of Chinese handmade papers routinely used to separate dishes in shipping. There are also drawers of tear sheets and old prints (the good and the not so good), antique cards and old letters and stamps, gift-wraps, stickers and cards, and old and torn drawings rescued from oblivion at secondhand shops. A great

LEFT TO RIGHT

At Secondhand Rose, an antiques and collectibles shop in downtown Manhattan, Suzanne Lipschutz offers four long walls of fabulous papers from the past, with an emphasis on those from the 30s, 40s, and 50s.; at Lang/Robertson's office wallpaper samples fill six file cabinets; art papers and other interesting paper pieces are stored in flat files; Donna, Lucretia, and wallpaper mechanic Charlie Puzzo.

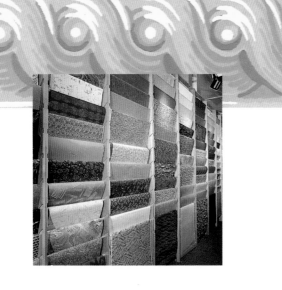

deal of this material has found its way into this book.

Decorating with Paper as a text was designed to touch upon many different materials, styles, and techniques. Certainly, commercially available wallpapers and borders were central to our selection process, since these are often the most easily come by. Of course, the choices available to us are extensive. We have professional access to hundreds of wholesale resources and the geographical advantage of living in a major metropolitan area where the unusual is as common as vin ordinaire. But no matter who you are

LEFT TO RIGHT

At Kate's Paperie, a Manhattan store specializing in fine paper goods, handmade papers are displayed on dowels; laser copies of valuable old prints closely mimic the originals; shaped boxes from Kate's Paperie are perfect bases for découpage; some of Hiram Mannings delicate cuttings; a selection of luxurious gold-leafed borders from Anya Larkin.

or where you live, there are thousands of beautiful commercially available wallpapers and other printed or plain papers that, when applied to the walls or to accessories, can turn a plain room or object into a magical one. There are also hundreds of borders that can be added to both accessories and walls. What we've specifically avoided using is what have come to be called "companion prints," or more simply, coordinates. Often a border will be bound right into a wallpaper book next to the matching "sidewall," or all-over print designed for the walls. Using papers and borders that come matched up like twin sets or limiting your choices in multipattern rooms to papers from a pre-edited "collection" can deprive you of the opportunity to pick something more unexpected and pleasing. We sincerely hope that the choices illustrated in this book will forever erase the notion that papers designed as coordinates are the only ones you should use together.

We have also presented a large selection of untraditional papers including handmades and gift-wraps, lowly wrapping papers, packing materials,

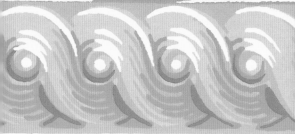

newspapers, gift cards, and the like. We doubt that many of you will choose to scour through your local equivalent of Chinatown ferreting out pieces of handmade packing materials to make a screen. But for the adventurous few, there is a broad assortment of unusual papers to pique your imagination.

We intentionally expanded the reach of the book from large to small projects, from the elaborate and time-consuming work of covering a room with cut flowers or Victorian prints to the simpler tasks of creating small paper-enhanced boxes or tabletop accessories. If your heart doesn't beat a little faster at the idea of découpaged lampshades, we've included more contemporary screens and boxes made from exquisite handmade Japanese papers combined with collected bits and pieces of memorabilia. These projects come in many different styles and shapes. And the ideas we've illustrated here can be adapted to nearly any style direction, so something we executed in kraft paper with applied fruits could be translated into marble paper with seashells or bright red Pantone with animals.

We hope that the philosophy of this book will liberate you from the "plain wall syndrome." Rooms with gorgeous window treatments and extraordinary furnishings can fall positively flat if the fabric patterns and the fine furniture are seen against plain painted walls. To our way of thinking, even a subtle textured paper is better than a bare wall.

An important and practical point is the issue of cost. Paper can be very affordable. In fact, a special paint job —one that includes meticulous preparation or sponging or glazes to add dimension to walls or ceilings—can cost much more than covering them in a basic textured paper. Certainly there are papers that cost three figures per roll. We use them often in our residential design work. Frequently, however, you can find copies of the more expensive papers that, once installed in the room, have a similar look with a much more palatable price tag. Much of what you will see photographed here is confined to the design trade. Please don't let that frustrate you into believing that the

look is unavailable to you without hiring a decorator. Check around. We are always pleasantly surprised at what is available through good paint and paper stores as well as mail-order sources. In fact, in many cases it's the identical stuff. Diverse and beautiful collections of papers from the most prestigious fabric and wallpaper design firms are sold in retail stores.

It's also important to mention early on that when dealing with most basic installations, the technical stuff is rather simple. There are various tools, several types of paste and glue, a few rules of thumb and sequence guides that can help avoid problems (all of which are described in the "Tools, Terms, and Techniques" chapters). You can pick up booklets on how to hang wallpaper at the paint store; they're usually thinner than a dime. Even professional paperhangers will tell you that although every job has its quirks, the basic stuff is pure kindergarten. It all depends on your level of confidence, how much

you want to try, how skillful your fingers are, and when and if you want to incorporate a professional into your renovation plans. You could, for example, hire a professional paperhanger to do the walls, which, although they can be the simplest part of the job, can also be very tricky. Lengths of paper are heavy, sometimes become fragile and tear when wet with paste, and require using ladders, levels, a lot of razor blades, and gigantic cutting tables. It might make more sense to have the pros haul the table and ladders to your home, paper the walls (and/or ceiling . . . particularly ceilings), clean up the mess, and leave, taking all the garbage to the proper disposal center. Then you can add your own particular genius with a border, or appliqués, or some other, smaller extension of the project. The cut-out and paste-on procedures in all the rooms we've photographed here were rather straightforward operations. You have to decide just how energetic you are and choose your level

of commitment accordingly.

Even though wallpaper isn't always a quick fix, the true and abiding beauty of paper is its incredible versatility. Because the raw edges will not fray, paper can be cut, assembled, glued one sheet to another, and applied on almost any surface you can dream up.

While we're on the subject of cutting and gluing and applying paper to paper, let's spend a few minutes on the meaning and use of the word *découpage* as it appears in this book. Découpage was popularized in eighteenth-century Europe and was developed into an extremely complicated art form by the very wealthy, for whom it was a favored pastime. In the traditional sense of the word, Donna and I are certainly not découpage artists, or, more accurately, *découpeures*. In fact, having spent many hours studying traditional découpage techniques, we learned that in the final analysis, this art form is far more demanding and time-consuming than is practical for our work and this book. Therefore, we will use the word frequently and talk about the craft aspects of découpage, but we are not talking about the traditional process. We who want to work room-sized (or quickly) need shortcuts.

The term *découpage*, however, as taken from the French word *découper*, to cut up or cut out, also describes the technique of simply decorating any surface with applied paper cutouts. Loosely interpreted, therefore, you can call work on a larger, room-sized scale, such as our little Greco-Roman sunroom, a "découpaged" room, or as we refer to it, "architectural découpage," in which architectural detail-

LEFT TO RIGHT

A fabulously découpaged bookcase in the home of Hiram Manning; trompe l'oeil plates line a mantel; meticulously hand-painted wallpapers in the studio of Anya Larkin; découpaged obelisque by Jered Holmes; scrap trunks epitomize the Victorian style of découpage.

ing is created by the application of cut papers. For work on this scale, we can't rely entirely on the complex traditional methods of découpage. We have interpreted these techniques, and through years of working with papers intended for use in interior decoration as well as some rather unconventional ones, a wide number of glues and adhesives, and a plethora of finishing and sealing materials and techniques, we've developed a completely fresh approach that combines the techniques of basic wallpapering and découpage. What we have here is the spirit of découpage without a lot of the fuss.

Traditional découpage also relied extensively on the use of original art and old, sometimes hand-colored prints, which, by painstakingly peeling away layers of paper from the back, were thinned down and then applied directly to surfaces. With fine prints becoming increasingly rare and costly, this book offers a twentieth-century alternative to using such prints directly. Color copies made on high-tech laser machines work beautifully for both old and new elements, allowing them to be duplicated endlessly for the creation of full borders out of separate elements, for example, without losing the originals. There are ingenious ways to use duplication to enhance your projects, both small and large.

Combining our knowledge of both the sealants used in traditional découpage and those not-so-traditional ones that work in interior decoration, we'll offer advice to help you decide when it's necessary to seal your work under coats of varnish, polyurethane, or a spray finish, when you should final-coat a piece with paste wax, and when you can leave well enough alone. The sealant we use most often is polyure-thane, both oil and latex versions. We also use varnish, both plain and tinted, to "age" prints or papers. For more information on sealants, look in the "Tools, Terms, and Techniques" chapters at the back of the book.

In our previous decorating book, *Decorating with Fabric*, we suggested that you consider Lang/Robertson your consulting interior design firm and our book the beginning of our client/designer relationship. We extend that invitation to you again. Certainly you alone know the requirements of lifestyle, budget, and design preferences that will influence your project and material choices. And while we will probably never have the opportunity to meet you and share directly in your creative process, we sincerely hope that our enthusiasm for the projects featured in this book and for the art and craft of using papers in the decoration of your home will encourage you to discover the pleasure of the hands-on approach to decorating. Decorating isn't just for professionals. You can be your own professional. Be bold! Be fearless! Try out combinations on your worktable. Forget the rules. And if all else fails, send us a swatch of what you're considering and we'll give you some help. Above all, don't be afraid to let your imagination fly. By deciding to try any of the ideas in this book, you are not committing your lifetime allotment of spare time. Using the information we provide and the rooms we've photographed as inspiration, you can make beautiful changes in your home that will continue to excite and please you for a long, long time to come. Because the ideas in *Decorating with Paper* have only one real limitation . . . the limits of your own imagination.

THE HISTORY OF
WALLPAPER AND DÉCOUPAGE

Paper itself was first developed in second-century China. It traveled a long and circuitous route to Western Europe, becoming a luxurious addition to that culture by the middle of the twelfth century. French and Italian artisans soon began to produce it in greater quantities, and eventually papers hand-printed with wood blocks were applied to walls. These first laboriously manufactured wallpapers offered the possibility of decorating smooth wall surfaces without the cost of fabrics or tapestries, or the nuisance of hiring temperamental itinerant artists. Sometime in the seventeenth century, paper production crossed the Atlantic, and papers hand-printed with American colonial motifs became available for use where stenciling or murals were unavailable or undesirable.

Although fine examples of découpage exist from ancient China and Persia, it wasn't until the seventeenth century that the art began to gain popularity in Italy, where it was developed to replicate Oriental lacquerwork furniture. Interest in découpage spread in the early eighteenth century to France, Germany, and England, where various techniques for cutting out and applying original hand-colored prints to furniture and artifacts became popular among fine craftsmen and as a pastime for the idle rich. The apogee of découpage was in eighteenth-century Europe, where the craze for decoration swept all before it. Découpage as a decorative art was nearly lost after the guilds dissolved at the end of the century, but it was revived with renewed enthusiasm in the mid-nineteenth century when Victorian ladies and gentlemen began to use precolored prints and pictures, combining them into interesting compositions, trimming them with gold paper braid, and applying them to practically everything. As découpage came into vogue again in the 1950s and early 60s, the list of desirable materials expanded to include gift cards, calendar art, pages torn from books and magazines, gift-wraps—all sorts of printed materials, whether colored, sepia, or black-and-white. Both the classic eighteenth- and nineteenth-century découpage work and the more contemporary versions, however, required extremely fine cutting and gluing, all performed within a rather specific set of technical rules and finished with many coats of varnish or other sealants, applied to bury the cut pieces in protective layers.

Découpaged furnishings and accessories have always had a special allure in interior decoration, adding a charming personal touch to a room. Recently, however, a resurgence of interest in découpage, both old and new, has been evident throughout the home furnishings and design market.

PART 1

ARCHITECTURAL EFFECTS AND DECORATIVE DETAILS

Through the magic of printed papers, you can transform your living room into a gazebo, create a marble and granite temple fit for a Roman emperor where an ordinary dining room once sufficed, or devise an elaborately detailed sunroom strewn with blossoms and trailing vines. Wallpapers and borders offer a nearly endless variety of textures and patterns and, when assembled with courage and panache, make a compelling and highly personal visual statement.

In this section we focus on wall work, from the most elaborate and intricately "constructed," rooms that are designed to create the illusion of architecture where none exists, to those enhanced by delicate textural papers, which add grace and elegance without pattern. We will also offer you an abundance of borders, some used singly and simply, and some layered and madly construed. There are styles both formal and relaxed, some stark and some embellished. Surely there will be several that catch your eye and change the way you think about wallpaper forever.

Decorative Wall and Border Treatments

Imagine walls made of paper bags, carefully colored and crushed
to create the illusion of ancient stone. Or striped walls bordered with
the same stripe placed (surprise!) on the diagonal. Or leopard walls,
goatskin walls, glazed-paper walls, walls of lattice, vines, and
blossoms, all detailed with fabulous borders and individual elements you
have assembled and applied in surprising and innovative ways.
Wallpapers were, of course, invented for walls, but you can reinvent

them with clever combinations, untraditional choices, and creative applications. Assuming that you understand the technical boundaries and heed the caveat of trying out layers or applications on scrap before committing to the walls themselves, you can dream up your own spectacular solutions and turn rooms into magical spaces full of the color and pattern of your own devising.

How to select a wallpaper

One could literally write a book on the subject of wallpaper selection. As interior designers we're called upon to help our clients choose from a seemingly limitless range of beautiful papers. But since there are thousands of papers out there (which means that even by conservative estimates, there are probably a dozen perfect ones for every job), it's a complicated process, even for pros. Just what makes one paper more perfect than another has to do with cost, the use for which it is intended, the condition of the walls, and, of course, personal taste. There are papers so tough that they are nearly indestructible and some so fragile that they stain if a drop of paste touches the surface during application. There are relatively inexpensive papers and there are others that cost several hundred dollars per roll or panel. There are dimensionally textured, heavy, and canvas-backed papers designed to disguise rough walls, and there are papers so thin that the slightest lump or bump on the bare wall surface becomes an eyesore in the finished room.

Then, of course, there are all those patterns to consider. There are stripes, florals, geometrics, novelties, all of

A medium-scale lattice print makes a beautiful mixer. We combined a soft blue lattice on a stippled ground with a flower and fruit swag border to detail a tiny kitchen eating area. The straight bottom of the swag border was trimmed away to create a scalloped edge. Then we cut out individual elements of the border paper, rearranged them, and glued them to the walls to create fruit and flower appliqués, from which a collection of old framed botanicals were hung. All of these little elements work effectively together because the space is also small.

which can range from the oversized to the minuscule. There are fabulous fakes that re-create the look of log cabins, ivy- or flower-covered gazebos, mosques, and castles; there are printed paper versions of silk moiré, crinkled and draped fabric, and myriad marbles and stones. There are papers created from real elements such as grass, feathers, and leaves. There are textured papers galore. There are glazed papers that look like expensively striéd, combed, and overpainted walls. The lists seem endless. Our wallpaper files extend for twenty-five feet, and those selections have been edited down from the vast array in the market to include only those we really love.

Occasionally a client will remain unconvinced that the paper we've selected for a particular room is the best one out there and will ask to be taken into the designer showrooms for another look around. After just a few stops our client is so completely confused by the options and alternatives that he or she will generally opt to quit looking and trust us. With all those possibilities, how can we help you to make the decision between stripe A and stripe B, the big floral and the little floral, the scenic and the strié? With some practice and careful consideration, you can learn to make very good stylistic choices, but before you fall hopelessly in love with *any* paper, you should take a hard look at the pragmatic factors.

First is likely to be the issue of cost. Of course, to know the real cost of using a particular paper, you must have a good idea of just how many rolls you will need. For that, use the information we offer on calculating rollage on page 191 or consult a professional paperhanger. If you have chosen not to do the installation yourself, you will also have to figure in the expense of having some-

A FEMININE BEDROOM

We papered this room in one of our favorites, a beautiful soft blue lattice sidewall that adds pattern and color to the wall without making too many visual demands. Printed in flat pigment white over a darker ground, this paper is produced in England and lightly sealed with a wipeable finish, making it a good choice for a bedroom or a room that doesn't get heavy use.

ROMANTIC DETAILS

The woman who lives in this home is a real buttons-and-bows, pattern-on-pattern person. To her, the freshly papered walls longed for additional details. Fortunately, paper allows you to build the decoration one step at a time. The leafy border, appliquéd paper ribbons and bows, and a group of lovely découpaged accessories add intricacy and charm to the room, above.

TEXTURED LIVING ROOM

This living room, nearly square and with only one window, is papered with a beautifully textured paper in a palomino beige. The paper looks crumbled on the roll and, when applied flat to the wall, keeps all of the little lines and wrinkles and the nuances of color. As originally designed in Italy, these textured papers are traditionally sealed after installation by the application of a thin coat of paste wax mixed with turpentine and linseed oil and buffed to a soft shine. We just couldn't find a paper installer crazy enough to handle this volatile mixture and so chose to leave the paper matte and unsealed. We have since learned, however, that using a soft paste wax can achieve very similar results without the risk of explosion and have successfully waxed walls and ceilings on other projects. Look in the "Tools, Terms, and Techniques" chapters for more information on waxing walls and ceilings.

If you look closely, you will undoubtedly notice the visible seams. Because this paper is hand-painted, the color tends to pool lightly at the edges, thereby exaggerating the seams. To help disguise this problem, every other panel was reversed and hung upside down. This room is a good example of careful placement of panels to make the visible seams part of the overall design.

one else hang the paper, a figure that usually is computed by the number of rolls. Fees vary widely, and it's a good idea to get a few estimates before you commit to one installer, or "mechanic," as they're called in the design business. If you *are* going to hang the paper yourself, you'll need to figure in the cost of the prep coats, adhesives, and any tools you will have to buy. If the total cost of the paper you'd love to see in the guest room is the equivalent of a year of private school tuition, keep looking. Many expensive papers have been replicated in less expensive versions and offer the look of the original for a substantially smaller investment.

Second, consider the end use of the paper. Obviously kitchens and busy hallways require a sturdy paper; bedrooms and dining rooms may not. The basic ground rules of maintenance should be dealt with early on in the selection process. You can have papers chemically treated to make them washable and moisture-proof, but it is a rather costly process and won't ever turn a fragile paper into one you can wisely install over the stove.

Third, you must also come to terms with the condition of the walls. If you choose a paper that will show every flaw in the wall beneath, a layer of liner paper may be necessary, thereby increasing your investment. Some walls will never work well under paper because of high moisture or heavy, textured plaster, for example. You might be better off putting papers on accessories, like screens, and just painting the walls a beautiful color.

After you have dealt with the issues of cost, maintenance, and wall condition, how can you make a good stylistic choice? If you know what *feeling* you want the finished room to have, you can look for a paper that will contribute to

LEOPARD-PRINTED FOYER

This city apartment, located in a fabulously detailed landmark Victorian building, is on a low floor, and the lack of direct sunlight combined with the mahogany and oak doors, moldings, and floors made it very somber. Rather than forcing white or pastel colors into the rooms in what we felt would be a futile effort to brighten them, we chose to accentuate the mysterious dark tones.

The ceilings in this apartment are 14 feet high, and since the rooms are small, the ceilings appeared even higher. It was necessary to break the walls into smaller sections in order to restore the scale of the rooms. Here in the foyer, we selected a dramatic paper, a leopard-printed vinyl in brown, Indian red, emerald green, and black with touches of metallic gold. The natural oak doors and moldings are such strong design elements that they lend a natural, warm dimension to the theatrics of the paper and tone down the impact of the print. By running the paper horizontally across the frieze and painting the plaster bottom molding to look like the wood, we lowered the ceiling height without making too much fuss about it. The brilliance of a gold-leaf paper turns the dark ceiling into a reflective glow of light. To brighten the long wall and relieve the darkness of the paper, we hung a collection of hand-colored Italian bird etchings in gilt frames. Even though the leopard paper has a lot of color when you isolate it, in this foyer it becomes an interesting but noncompetitive background for the architecture, furnishings, and accessories.

that effect. You can create a bower of
roses in a bedroom, for example, and
then complete your private garden with
floral or flower-colored upholstery. You
can put crisp, bright stripes in a sunny
room or a dark and dramatic paisley in
a room with heavy wood furniture and
no direct sunlight at all. You can paper
the ceiling of a paneled library so that
it becomes integrated into the room
rather than floating into off-white
never-never land. You can make the
walls the background or the star.

Look closely at the rooms photographed in this book, marking those
that appeal strongly to you; analyze
them, and note just what it is you like
about the way the papers work in those
rooms. Focus on the walls and imagine
them with your collection of artwork,
furniture, and accessories; otherwise
you may face a sizable additional investment. Remember, within every decorating style there are many beautiful
paper choices; limiting yourself to a
group that is compatible with your pos-
sessions won't limit your creativity to
any large degree.

Considering maintenance and stain-resistance treatments

The issue of wallpaper maintenance
must be dealt with early on in the deci-
sion-making process. Maintenance is a
very real, practical concern and there
are many situations in which maintenance problems must affect your choice
of papers. Fact: Small children with
peanut butter on their fingers will de-
stroy unprotected papers around light
switches within minutes of their installation. Scrubable vinyls are the best
choice for rooms inhabited by tots.
Fact: Kitchens are no place for a delicate

hand print that has not, at the very least, been treated to be "wipeable" (which is not, please note, the same thing as "scrubable"; paper samples should come marked with those terms right on the back). Fact: Bathrooms always raise the nasty issues of moisture and mildew. Papers installed inside shower or tub enclosures, like Newton's apple, will come down. They may also streak with mildew. If you choose to paper in damp spaces, buy extra. You may need it.

However, we do frequently disregard these caveats. Never having seen an indestructible paper that didn't look as if it belonged in the Bates Motel, we often find ourselves counseling a client to accept a moderate amount of risk taking when the paper is perfect for the space. Untreated papers can be protected to some degree by one of several stain-resistance techniques. There are companies that specialize in chemically treating papers to be stain-repellent and washable, thus turning fragile papers into more durable ones. This process makes the paper waterproof so that liquids bead up on the surface rather than being absorbed and staining the paper. Some European papers are colored with tempera (watercolor) paints and even the adhesive can, if it touches the face, stain the paper as it is hung. These papers absolutely require treatment before installation. Since we frequently use untreated, delicate papers in our design work, we routinely send rolls out to be treated before they are installed. This conforms to the old adage "Better safe than sorry," and even though it adds considerably to the purchase price, it gives the paper a longer wall life.

There are products on the market that are designed to clean wallpapers. They are puttylike dry-cleaners that work like erasers, absorbing dust and

PEARLESCENT TEXTURE

Because of the pearlescent finish coat, which catches and magnifies the light, the gray-green paper in the room takes on a special glow at night. The warmth from the incandescent lights glistens along the textured surface, transforming the room. All colors change to some degree in artificial light, of course, so it is always a good idea to consider paper choices in the actual room at various times during the day and night, on sunny and cloudy days, before selecting one you will live with for many years.

dirt from the surface. Some are recommended for paper lampshades, window shades, and blinds as well as walls. Absorbene, the one we use for small spots and soil, has been around, unchanged, since 1891.

Many years ago, we worked frequently with an elderly and widely experienced German painter and paperhanger who shared his Old World paper cleaning trick with us. "Just take a wad of raw rye bread dough, make it into a ball, and wipe it across the soiled area of the paper," Heinz used to say, nodding his head up and down knowingly. It is a fascinating idea, but we suspect we'll never know for sure if Heinz was pulling our leg or letting us in on one of the ten great secrets of the universe.

Using textural papers

Recently the market has seen a strong influx of textured, or "special effects," papers that rather than bringing distinctive prints or motifs into the design scheme, simply add surface interest and visual depth. Patterned papers can be intrusive and demanding; but textural papers are backgrounds and, as such, allow other elements in the room to take center stage.

When the solid tone of a painted wall isn't quite interesting enough but the cost of artistic faux finishes applied with paint are beyond your budget, textured papers can be the perfect solution. These papers, which have a subtle all-over pattern designed to resemble multi-layers of color or a small-scale texture, can look rather unassuming on the roll. When they are applied to the walls, however, they add depth to the basic color palette and give the illusion of an elaborately detailed wall. In most

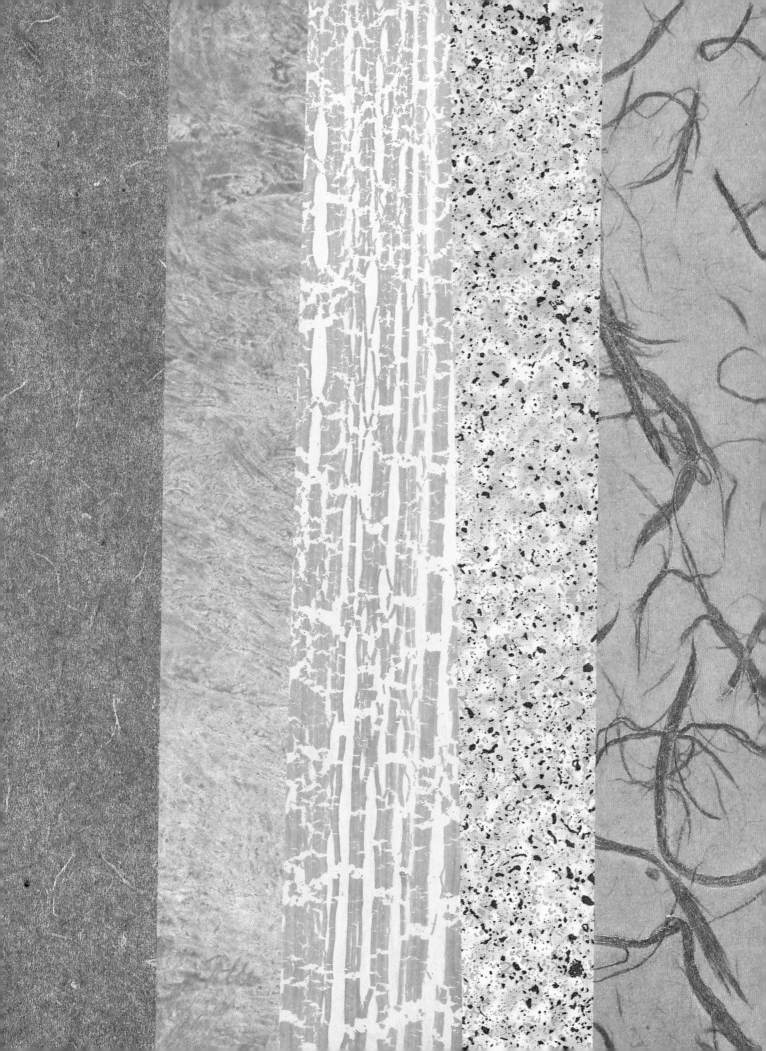

BORDERED BEDROOM

This modest, lightly patterned paper provides a quiet texture in the room, adding interest without fanfare, while the border gives oomph to the undistinguished crown molding. The scroll motifs on the border were placed directly over the beds, and a deliberate attempt was made to line them up in an understandable way with the seams of the paper. Places where this alignment was impossible were preplanned to fall in areas where the furniture or window treatment disguised and therefore minimized them.

cases, they are designed to resemble materials other than paper: leather, goatskin, suede, marble, granite, malachite and other semiprecious stones, sponged walls, glazed walls, combed walls, striés, moirés, and so on.

Particularly when used in combination with borders, these papers add great style without aesthetically dominating the room. The downside of these marvelous papers is that they may leave you with undisguised seams, which in busier patterns can get lost in the print. In some cases, in fact, the seams will be very demanding and will, by virtue of their strong vertical lines, become part of the design scheme of the room. In nearly all installations using these papers, you will see the seams, which of course is not the case with painted walls. We are of the opinion, however, that seams, whether very apparent or more quietly visible, are part of the honesty of papered walls and should be accepted and not fretted over. Of course, the quality of the installation will greatly affect the finished look of your seams. There are techniques that minimize the seams but they do require some skill and might, in fact, necessitate a professional installer. In general, the busier the texture, the less apparent the seams will be in the finished room.

Using wallpaper borders

BORDERED LOFT

In this city loft belonging to Libby Cameron of Parish Hadley Associates a traditional swag border was applied to the painted walls, creating a fresh and rather unexpected design detail. The border runs throughout the apartment, uniting various living areas with its common thread.

Just from flipping through this book, it should be obvious immediately that Lang/Robertson loves borders. We use them so frequently that we routinely start a design project by selecting an interesting border or borders. There are several very good reasons for this. First, borders can provide architectural details in a room with few or none. They make excellent "crown mold-

CHEERFUL LIVING ROOM

This wallpaper is of a type called "strié," or striped; it replicates the look of an expensive glazed wall that would have been striéd with a tinted glaze coat. The raised finish makes the paper more interesting than a flat paper; however, be aware that everything applied over the paper will show the striping.

The special touch in this room comes from a panel-printed paper from Brunschwig & Fils that features "faience" pottery in a style called "Luneville." We cut out the individual motifs and applied them to the wall above the mantel, creating the illusion of assorted pieces lined up casually against the wall. Several real pieces on the mantel add to the illusion.

Since the high ceilings allowed us to use a very wide border, we were able to combine two bold ones; although they come from different resources they complement each other and appear as one. Cutting out the tassels in the lower of the two borders caused them to appear so three-dimensional that they fool the eye. Besides adding a lushness to the design, the colorful border ties the walls to the fabrics by repeating the roses and accenting the dark notes in the prints.

ings," for example, visually separating the ceiling from the walls without the fuss and expense of carpentry. They also add another touch of color to a room. For instance, repeating some of the fabric colors up along the ceiling line is a charming way to add vitality to the room. Borders also offer the possibility of mixing in another pattern, which of course multiplies the visual "layers" in a room, adding to the interest and complexity of the decoration. In rooms where elaboration is a theme, borders around ceiling lines, doors, and windows—even on the ceiling—all contribute to an orchestrated mix of color and pattern.

However, we look at a printed border as merely a beginning, a starting place. Cutting into the border, combining it with others, doubling it up, all of these tricks unlock new possibilities and allow us to use the border to its fullest advantage in the room. Nearly every border is printed with a straight edge along the top and bottom of the pattern, allowing you to trim it easily with a straight edge or large shears. Often, however, the border can be greatly enhanced by careful trimming *into* the pattern along the bottom, thereby creating an irregular bottom edge. This technique integrates the border into the wall color or pattern, attractively softening the look of the room design.

CUSTOMIZING BORDERS

Borders come in hundreds of styles and patterns and in a wide variety of colors and widths. Some borders are architectural by design; that is, they give the illusion of real architectural detail and can be used very effectively in place of crown moldings, baseboards, window and door frames, and other such wood or plaster trim. These borders are generally intended to have a straight bottom edge, much as a real wood or plaster trim would have. Other borders, however, can be customized by cutting into the border in an interesting way. Bows, ribbons, clusters, flowers, shells, and the like can be cut out for individual appliquéing to extend the border into the ground paper. Our favorites are florals, which, although they nearly always come with a printed line along the bottom edge, are more beautiful when the straight edge is cut away, allowing the outlines of the petals and leaves to create an irregular bottom edge. Here are some ideas and tips for customizing borders:

▪ Cutting away the bottom edge of a border by following the printed motifs will integrate the border into the wallpaper, creating a more interesting, livelier pattern against the wall and eliminating the barrier of the straight bottom edge.

▪ In rooms with undistinguished crown moldings or no moldings at all, doubling the border along the ceiling line adds architectural interest and visual importance.

▪ Try "mirroring" a border by placing it on the walls along the ceiling line and then duplicating it on the ceiling. With some border patterns, this can give a "lift" to the ceiling. Be careful to match the main pattern motifs on both the walls and the ceiling. Since you will have to miter the pattern at the corners on the ceiling, it may throw off the match slightly.

▪ To combine borders, you need designs that are compatible, though not necessarily ones that were printed to go together (called "companion" papers). Look carefully at many resources to find borders that work together, and try combining florals with ribbons, stars with stripes, fringes with bird's nests . . . whatever you find that looks good to you!

▪ If you are creating a border from many separate elements, use a nonpermanent, nonoily clay like Plasti-Tak to temporarily hold the individual pieces on the wall while you finalize your design. You can then glue them in place one by one. A small vinyl smoother is an excellent tool for pushing excess adhesive out from under the border and securing all the little edges. Work over the border until it is firmly in place. Tiny pieces may lift as the border dries, requiring a little more glue and some patience. Always use border adhesive to apply borders since no other adhesive will give you a guaranteed bond. Clean up immediately and well since border adhesive, once dried, becomes impossible to remove.

BED OF ROSES

When interior designer Barbara Lazarus determined the placement of this strong floral pattern, she took special care to position the panels so that the main motif was centered in such critical places as the bed wall and over the fireplace. This floral has a large repeat and a half-drop (see page 191) and therefore required considerable additional rollage.

PLACING A PATTERN EFFECTIVELY IN A ROOM

Before you put a dab of paste on a single strip of paper, you should have determined just where you want the print, the panels, and the seams to fall in the room. Here are some guidelines to help you make placement decisions:

- To make planning easier, use four pieces of graph paper and lay out each wall to scale, indicating all door and window openings. Then lay the four drawings, called elevations, side by side in the proper order. Mark the elevation of the most visible and important wall in the room. Still working in the scale of your drawings, cut out several strips of tracing paper the width of your wallpaper and place them over the wall elevations, starting on the main wall and trying out several placement plans to see what happens at the corners.

- Generally, you will want to center either a seam or the center of a panel on each wall, depending on what happens in the corners. Very narrow strips at the two outside edges of a wall are unappealing and should be avoided.

- Strongly printed papers should be placed attractively on all the main walls, but they should also run around the room as if they were continuous. This isn't always easy or possible; some rooms allow you few or no placement choices. You can cheat a little in the corners, trimming off a bit where it is unlikely to be noticed. Most rooms have one corner, called a "blind" corner, selected because it's behind a door or a curtain, where the pattern doesn't have to match at all.

- Even though you want the paper to appear to run around the room in one continuous piece, you must always cut the paper at both inside and outside corners. Sheetrock and plaster are rarely perfectly straight, and therefore the pattern will distort or fall away from perfect vertical, and the paper will pull away from the corner in places, wrinkle, and look sloppy. Refer to the section on papering corners on page 198.

- Using a textured paper where the seams will be visible is nearly the same as using a paper with a strong pattern. You will have to place the seams intelligently in the room so that they look deliberate and not random.

- When using large, demanding prints, it is wise to order an extra double roll. This allows you some flexibility in the final placement of the panels during installation.

- With small all-over prints, you can design the placement of the seams on a wall-by-wall basis as long as you don't leave any really narrow strips at the sides.

- If you are planning to use a panel print, a design that must be placed in sequence to create a scene or mural, predetermining placement before buying the paper is crucial. In some rooms, panel prints just cannot be used because they will be too broken up by doors, windows, or the height of the wall. Bear in mind, though, that you can request extra rolls of the ground paper to fill in short or awkward spaces on the walls or over doors or windows.

CREATING PRINT ROOMS

Print rooms were popular in eighteenth- and nineteenth-century England, where they served as charming exhibit rooms for prints. An unusual way for those returning from grand tours abroad to display a sort of souvenir album of visited landmarks, print rooms often featured engravings of favored classical ruins and city scenes. Rather than being framed and hung from hooks, the prints were glued right onto beautifully colored walls or paneling and then "framed" with printed paper frames. Other appliqués, including cords and tassels, rosettes, garlands, and chains, were applied, adding to the illusion of an attractively arranged collection of carefully selected, framed art. Along with engravings of cities and classical ruins, hunt scenes and botanicals became frequent themes. Usually quite small and intimate, these intriguing rooms were set like little jewels in the vast houses of the wealthy and prominent.

Print rooms require laborious preparation of the walls or wood surfaces and are, in fact, frequently built over canvas, which is applied like liner paper over the repaired, washed, and prepped walls. Since they are enormously time-consuming and difficult to create, print rooms demand perfect surfaces. Although reproductions will work well, an authentic print room uses real prints rather than copies and is, therefore, an expensive undertaking. Some feature collections of black-and-white prints, some sepia, some hand-colored; some use combinations of these. The planning of the room—selecting prints, arranging them on the walls or panels, locating and cutting out all the frames and details—was a pleasant diversion for English ladies and gentlemen. The process retains its allure even after several centuries.

Recently, kits for creating print rooms have become available, offering interesting examples of all of the frame and detailing elements printed in black-and-white and easily reproduced on a standard copier. All you need to add are the prints and creative energy.

THE PRINT ROOM

This small entry room, created by English artist Nicola Wingate Saul, is a perfect example of a classic eighteenth-century English-style print room. These walls were meticulously prepared, then primed and painted, and finally glazed to tone down the rawness of the yellow walls and lacquer green woodwork, giving the whole room a soft patina. The prints were arranged wall by wall with careful attention to the overall balance of the room, with no wall visually stronger than another.

Architectural Découpage

Typically, homes come with uninspiring blank walls,

unornamented windows and doorways, and in most cases, a total lack

of interesting architectural detail. No elegant crown moldings.

No dadoes. No carving. Looking at this from the most positive point

of view, it presents you with the perfect "dress it up,

dress it down" environment. If, however, in your wildest fantasies

you've longed to live in a Renaissance palace or a neoclassical temple

TROMPE L'OEIL DETAIL
The neoclassical urn and the architectural detail, part of a collection reproduced from fine old prints by J. Pocker & Son, offer an amusing trompe l'oeil distraction on the sunroom walls. The plinth was actually trimmed from a large structural detail, originally copied from Roman ruins.

CREATING (IMPORTANT) MOLDINGS, *PREVIOUS PAGE*
Because this sunroom has no crown moldings at all, we added a lightweight cardboard and foam cove molding at the ceiling line. This changed the feeling of the room instantly, visually lifting the ceiling and giving the room a new elegance. The cove was then papered and further detailed with borders, and a final strip of border was glued onto the actual ceiling surface. The illusion is really show-stopping. No one who visits this room can believe that there's nothing overhead but paper and paste!

complete with marble walls, columns, pilasters or pediments surrounding doorways or windows, a frieze of nymphs and satyrs, and elaborate dentil moldings, you can create the illusion with paper. You can turn a plain wall into a wall of *boiserie* (the French word for elegant wood paneling), add a chair rail or wainscotting on walls or ceiling, create any ambience from a Brighton pavilion built of lattice to a log cabin—all with paper. The simplest of rooms can become evocative of another era, another lifestyle, another income bracket. Perhaps the rooms photographed here represent a more stylized look than you'd want for your own home, but our intention is to illustrate the ultimate fantasy of cut paper that might inspire you, should you have the time and inclination, to undertake to create a masterpiece of what we call "architectural découpage."

It was inevitable that the fascination with nineteenth-century neoclassicism in the late 1980s would cause a proliferation of papers designed to duplicate the building and ornamental materials of that period. The market was primed for more faux-finish papers, and new groups of faux marbles, granites, and stones along with the addition of scores of frieze, cornice, dado, and other molding borders came as no surprise. Stone lions, gargoyles, and Greco-Roman heads and statues appeared in nearly every major resource collection. Papers suitable for simulating architectural details had existed, of course, but they were mainly conceptual, not literal. This influx of printed architecture was fresh and exciting. Paper offered limitless opportunity for grandiose ornament, requiring no wood-carvers, no stonemasons, no plasterers. In its way, this trend offered a bold update on print rooms—intricate, intellectual, creatively stimulating ways to use paper to create fantasy rooms that were highly personalized, required considerable time and patience, and were meant to be enjoyed in large part for themselves rather than as backgrounds for furniture, art, and accessories.

By far the most elaborately detailed room we've ever designed was a sunroom created for a designer showhouse. It was our first choice of the various rooms offered to designers because it was a perfect blank canvas for the style we had in mind: it was nearly square, had a feeling of openness, had dramatic arched windows, and featured an old terrazzo floor. The terrazzo had been poured when the house was built in the late 1800s and had worn over the years to a beautiful, soft, weathered gray-beige. As is often the case, the existing elements in the room determined our color and design scheme.

Our idea was to create a sort of tongue-in-cheek Greco-Roman temple, done in soft marble and stone colors and incorporating some elements of traditional Greek and Roman architecture in an untraditional way. For this, a perfect border paper existed in the market. It was called "Erectheum" and was based on those wonderful standing ladies in elegant robes (called caryatids) that served as columns surrounding the exterior of the Erectheum on the Acropolis in Athens. It came with a separate border that made a perfect faux-stone dado molding around the room. Of course, the distance between the caryatids on the printed border didn't space perfectly on the four walls of our sunroom. In order to keep the look of the border while accommodating the actual room measurements, we decided to cut out the individual caryatids and use them where they would be used in a real structure to carry the weight: under the

PLACING THE MOTIFS

Here our little caryatids, positioned as they would be in a real structure (at the corners, under the window frames, and alongside the doorways), flank a griffin panel. By using the border both on the walls and on the dado in this way, the many elements that are used in this room are joined by a common design thread. The result is harmonious and beautiful.

SEAMLESS EXECUTION

When we planned this wall on graph paper, we sketched several different ways to position the seams of the faux-marble wallpaper, trying to choose a way that would be the least noticeable on this wall where no furniture distracts the eye. Since the horizontal "granite" panels would be glued over the faux-marble sidewall, we could minimize the disruption by aligning the seams of the marble paper with the outside edge of the border on the granite panels. To do this, we planned a seam at the center of the wall and then cheated a little by trimming the first set of panels, slated to go to the right and to the left of the center, narrowing each by a few inches. The first seam, therefore, is centered (where it is nearly hidden by the mirror); the second set of seams lines up with the outside of the border and looks intentional; and the third set of seams occurs over each of the doors. In tricky installations like this, careful and creative planning is a prerequisite.

windows, in the corners, and alongside the doors. By using the border elements where we needed them, gluing them on the all-over marble paper with which we had covered all the walls, we were, in effect, creating our own border.

Once we'd decided to free the little paper ladies from their background, all sorts of other possibilities opened up. We found a paper that included a version of baroque grotesques, these in the form of fantasy lion heads on plaques. It, too, came in a gray-beige colorway, although not identical to the colors in the caryatid border. But, as often happens, the fact that they didn't exactly match made the mix more lively and interesting. We used them to create granite "panels" over the marble base paper, which broke into the larger wall spaces in a way that gave more weight and importance to the individual lions and caryatids.

Printed in the spaces between the caryatids on the Erectheum border were griffins, those medieval fantasy animals that decorated the flying buttresses in Gothic architecture. We had put them aside as we cut. Freely chopping into the papers now, we clipped the griffins out in rectangles that perfectly fit the spaces between the caryatids, thereby allowing us the freedom to center them on each wall and under each window. Designing the room in this way, wall by wall, was not unlike creating a four-part collage; each wall was a separate picture, but each had to relate to both its own architectural requirements, such as the doors and windows, and the other three walls. As we worked, cutting and trying, discarding, looking through various papers and borders for elements we could successfully incorporate, the floor became littered with bits and pieces of cut-out paper. What was missing was one strong element that we could use to pull all these separate, slightly mismatched pieces together into one harmonious room.

The answer came in the form of a narrow strip cut from a larger border, which we used to outline both the panels we'd applied over the "marble" walls and the griffin panels. It was a simple gimmick that caused the walls to appear three-dimensional, as if they had been cut from stone. (Just for the record, the marble sidewall, the granite in the panels, and the little outlining border came from three separate wallpaper resources.) By using this one integrating border element over and over again in the room, any inconsistencies among the papers were minimized, and rather than a mad assemblage of bits and pieces, the room was made to appear as a unified whole.

By the time we had made our final selections, designing the room and its papered furnishings (the room screen and the tabletop), we had used fourteen different papers from five different resources. This sunroom is the ultimate example of just what magic can be performed with printed paper.

Nearly all of what we developed in our sunroom had been brewing over a period of several years. The first time we layered papers to create a feeling of architectural detail was in 1987 in a tiny elevator in a wonderful beach house. The elevator provided us with the perfect opportunity to create something a little wild and crazy within a large off-white contemporary home. Using several different colorways of the same pattern and a border designed to complement (but not match) them, we sectioned the walls to create brightly contrasting panels. Because the papers all came from the same collection, the risks weren't high, and it was a fun and unexpected change of pace from the rest

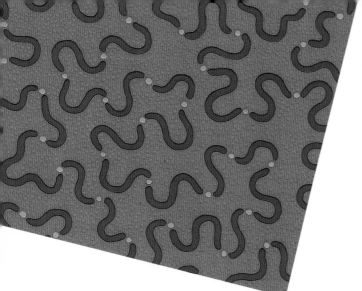

ELABORATELY PAPERED ELEVATOR

Because this elevator was a tiny space and was hidden behind a closed door almost all of the time, we decided to make it a big surprise. The house is classical and restrained; the elevator is papered in a wild little squiggle print from the Zandra Rhodes collection at Osborne & Little. The house has "serious" art; the elevator has childlike colored etchings. All that contrast makes for energized design and good fun.

of this cool and collected residence.

In 1989 we were asked to redecorate the foyer of Boussac of France, the prestigious fabric and wallpaper firm. The task was to create something eye-catching and innovative. Designated as a display space, this showroom with its narrow foyer exists in a commercial building where there isn't a friendly detail to be found. We chose main patterns from one group of papers from the newest collection, but to the consternation of the Boussac staff, we insisted on venturing beyond this small group into others that were not part of the co-ordinated collection but had similar colorings and compatible designs. In this way we were able to expand the possibilities, incorporating a group designed to be used together but then adding papers that were slightly different, in both design and coloration.

The walls were all very different, both in length and in configuration. We had decided to approach the design of the space in the style of French boiserie, or wood paneling, and to elaborate each wall independently. The first necessity, therefore, was to graph out the individual walls to scale and determine how we could adjust the sizes of the interior panels on each wall in a way that would work comfortably with the adjoining one. Some panels would be large, some smaller, but all of them have the same basic elements, altered slightly to fit easily into the available space. This wall-by-wall plan would be necessary for each and every architecturally engineered space we would plan over the years. With the little elevator, we could hold up patterns and strips and make decisions on the spot. With larger, more complicated spaces, that was impossible. The only way was to make a master drawing of the individual walls on graph paper and then use tracing paper to sketch out possibilities. This process had to be successfully completed before we could even begin to determine how much of each paper we would need to order.

The main border we selected was printed as a companion for another paper, a large-scale leaf pattern featuring oriental motifs, which had a matching fabric. To create the look of boiserie, for our ground paper we decided on a soft taupe printed moiré that actually looked a bit like woodgrain. The moiré was applied to all the walls, floor to ceiling. Over this we applied the border along the ceiling line, using border adhesive to accommodate the vinyl over vinyl and help keep it from curling. Since we were working for the manufacturer and had the unusual luxury of virtually unlimited materials, we took the liberty of cutting thin strips from the top and bottom of the yards and yards of border to create the narrow outlines of all the wall panels. A third paper, a stripe that offered a compatible dark, narrow section that looked to us like a shadow, gave us the little strips of dark gray that frame the panels and the chair rail. The walls were nearly complete in this dramatic foyer before we selected the leopard print for the bottom panels. It's rarely wise to make all the decisions about a room before you start to install it. Even practiced professionals sometimes feel the need to let the room "grow" and, as a result, allow themselves some design flexibility right through the process. We call that sequential design thinking and believe that it's a sound way to work, particularly on difficult projects like this one. Nothing ever looks exactly the same when it goes up all around you, no matter how carefully you may have imagined it beforehand. The finished foyer, once an architecturally barren, Sheet-

PAPER-PANELED FOYER

A leopard-print paper we love and use frequently in its various color versions added just the right amount of punch to these faux-boiserie paneled walls. By incorporating a small amount of a dark and dramatic paper into the wall design, we acknowledged the black keys in the granite tile floor, the strong, jewel-toned découpaged tabletop on a black pedestal, and the black lacquer picture frame with its brilliantly colored ancestor art.

rocked commercial space, has become a jewel of an entryway, welcoming designers and clients.

Working with papers from many sources and working with a large group of companions and compatibles from one resource are two ways to approach architectural découpage. The third is to utilize a group of papers that provide all the needed architectural elements and borders as well as a sidewall, sold individually to accommodate varying room sizes and configurations but designed to create a particular architectural space. One of the prettiest is the gazebo print from Brunschwig & Fils.

The room we chose for these papers was nearly square. This allowed us to carry the gazebo illusion up and onto the ceiling, creating a partial roof. It was a difficult challenge to measure out the ceiling and determine the size and design of the roof, requiring careful drawings and some clever engineering of the available borders. By "engineering" we mean using the individual elements in combinations, either designed or fortuitous, to create believable, attractive solutions to the requirements of the room in a way that appears to be structural rather than purely decorative. This group of papers offered columns, capitals, and plinths as well as a border and a lattice sidewall. Allowing for individual adjustments necessary to adapt the pieces to the room, we "built" the gazebo, planning it wall by wall on graph paper.

If you look carefully, you'll be able to see how the different printed patterns were utilized. A section cut from the center of the printed columns, for example, was used on the ceiling to frame the edge of the gazebo "roof." The border was applied partially on the ceiling and partially on the crown molding, where it resembles a dentil molding.

GAZEBO ROOM

Our gazebo, created from a collection of papers from Brunschwig & Fils, was carefully engineered to duplicate the look of a real structure. We began by laying out all of the walls on graph paper, shifting the design possibilities around until the scheme worked on the drawing board. First the columns were positioned in the most logical way; true to their structural function, they appear to support the roof at key places around the room. The border runs around the room like a lintel, covering the actual crown molding. The ceiling paper, positioned to match the pattern on the walls as closely as possible, was designed with its open "roof" on the diagonal, a trick that creates both an interesting tension in the design and the illusion that the room is larger than it is in reality.

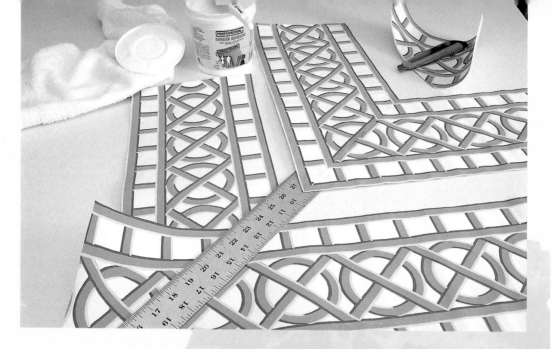

CREATING MITERED BORDERS

Miters are used to create attractive right angles. Most frequently, miters are necessary when borders intersect, such as around windows and doors, when creating wall panels, outlining the panels of a screen, making a picture mat, or decorating a frame, tray, box, etc. These are the steps to creating a perfect miter:

1. Determine where in the border pattern you can make the best and most visually effective diagonal seam. This is a matter of aesthetic preference and will vary from paper to paper, project to project. Usually you begin by placing the strongest element in the center of each side of your project (on a picture mat, you would have four sides; on a door, three sides; etc.) Check to see what happens in the corners; both the corners and the sides need to work in the most attractive and effective way. Sometimes you may have the option of designing the piece to comply with the most successful miter. If you have designed a screen that prominently uses a mitered edge on all the panels and the border miters

perfectly on a 16-inch-wide panel but is slightly off on an 18-inch-wide panel, you might choose to cut the panels 16 inches wide to ensure a good result.

2. Once you have decided where to place the pattern, cut strips for all the sides, leaving each one a little longer than you will actually need.

3. Put border adhesive on two intersecting strips and apply them on the surface, overlapping the right angle at the predetermined place on the pattern.

4. Using a new razor blade or craft knife and a metal ruler, triangle, or cutting edge, double-cut (see page 184) corner to corner on a 45-degree angle. You may be more comfortable cutting one piece at a time, using the first cut angle as a guide to cut the second and fine-tuning the match, but you must work quickly before the adhesive dries.

5. Pull out the excess from underneath and secure the pieces with a smoother or seam roller.

6. Carefully remove all excess adhesive with a clean damp sponge.

COORDINATING SCREEN
More of the assertive lattice print was used to cover a folding screen, framed with the same border used along the ceiling line and carefully mitered at the corners (see box on opposite page).

FIREBOX FACING
Looking convincingly like expensive marble, the tiles surrounding this firebox are, in fact, fabulous fakes. The old tiles were covered, one by one, with squares of pale green, self-adhesive marble paper, trimmed to allow the real grout to show. Soot from the fire has discolored some of the "tiles," adding to the illusion.

BASEBOARD DETAIL
To further enhance the illusion of a real structure, the columns that frame each window and door opening "support" the papered crown molding and rest squarely on the quarter-round molding at the floor line. Generously coating the paper column base detail with adhesive and allowing it to soak in for several minutes until it had softened made it much easier to sculpt over the actual baseboard.

Often rooms have architectural glitches that are easier to hide than change. This room had a window that was designed to open on a porch. When the porch was enclosed to make an office, the only place to put office bookshelves was against that window wall. Rather than make another set of curtains, we hid the window behind a screen. What this busy gazebo room didn't need was another pattern to add to the mix, however, so the screen was designed to blend attractively into the wall. To keep the screen interesting without adding too much jazz, the carefully mitered border was applied around the outside edges only, rather than around each panel.

One of the subtle problems you must confront when working with trompe l'oeil papers like these is the use of painted shadows which, although adding to the illusion of three-dimensionality, can sometimes determine the application. Patterns with shadows, for example, cannot be turned upside down and used in the same room, because the shadows will then appear on the wrong side of the "structure."

Architectural découpage unquestionably demands a huge commitment of time and effort, and a serious investment in paper as well. But you can create extraordinary spaces such as the ones pictured here, rooms that will excite you as much intellectually as they do aesthetically. Like a well-crafted novel, they can be full of little twists and turns, problems encountered and solved, nuances barely noticed because they are so successfully realized. Often in interior design the most harmonious and integral spaces belie an incredible effort. In these rooms, you can almost see the thinking, even as you enjoy their success.

COLUMNS DEFINE WINDOWS
We planned the placement of the lattice sidewall wallpaper on these walls starting from the "columns" on either side of the window and door openings. Because they rise from the floor to the papered crown molding, the columns effectively isolate all of the areas in between. The narrow strips of sidewall over and under the windows and doors were cut to center the pattern, not to match the sidewall as if it continued behind the columns.

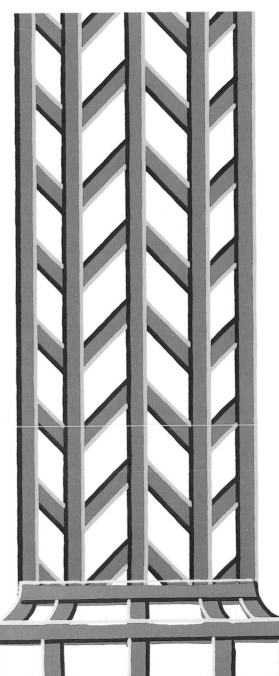

ENGINEERING ARCHITECTURAL PATTERNS

Altering, editing, and adjusting architectural patterns to fit a particular room require both creative thinking and careful planning. A good illustration for this concept is the Greco-Roman sunroom, pictured here in its four elevations (that is, the four individual walls seen straight on).

The papered room effectively disguises some very tricky design problems. For example, even though the room was nearly a perfect 16-foot square, since the window openings varied, there were small but difficult differences in the top third of the window and window/door walls. (Compare photographs #1 and #3.) The wall with one large window or window/door opening offered plaster wall space that was larger and of a different shape than that on the wall with two window openings. That occurred, of course, because of the difference in the curve of the larger and smaller window openings. How could we successfully paper those mismatched walls and integrate the discrepancies in a quiet but contributive way?

The wall space on the double window wall was too narrow to add a vertical panel, so we created two long horizontal panels across the wall as if the windows were not there. The two walls with a single window or window/door opening needed a pair of tall, thin panels to

complete them. This left, however, a space at the top corners of the window openings that, because it would not be hidden by the sheer curtains we had designed for the room, would look empty.

We decided that a triangular panel would fit nicely, but because of the shape of the space, it had to incorporate a *curved* bottom edge. The printed border, of course, was perfectly straight. Just as we had on the other walls, we cut the faux-granite paper into the panel shape, a triangle with a blunted long point and a curved bottom. Then we applied the two straight strips of the border. By carefully snipping into the bottom edge of a third piece of the border, making a ¼-inch clip every ½ inch along the bottom edge, we enabled the straight paper to be gently curved. After thoroughly saturating the clipped strip with adhesive to soften it, we placed it on the wall, gently easing it into the required curve. All the corners were then mitered. The results are splendid. Looking at it,

you'd never suspect that the paper wasn't printed in a perfectly matched curve!

Finally, the wall between the two doors was paneled with one set of faux-granite panels centered between. Since the doors were not equidistant from the corners, we left the little space to the right and left undecorated. The focus of this wall would be the mirror (see page 52); therefore the unequal spaces would not be noticeable.

Detailed Ceilings, Windows, and Doors

Ceilings, since they are uninterrupted by furniture, doors,

or windows, offer the largest blank space in a room and nearly endless

decorating possibilities. Applying paper by the roll, cut papers,

or borders can make your ceilings a contributive element of the

room design, adding shine, color, texture, or pattern. Windows that

frame lovely views and have some architectural character of their

own can be subtly enhanced by the addition of decorative borders

EXTRAVAGANT WINDOW CORNICE, *PREVIOUS PAGE*

These cornices were cut from plywood and then papered in a dark green-on-green stripe; a trimmed border; "lace" made from paper napkins; and flowers and ribbons cut from scraps and showroom samples.

or borders created from all-over patterns, replacing costly fabric window treatments. And doors—even hollow-core doors, perhaps the most uninspired wood item of all—can be cleverly trimmed with borders used alone over paint or in combination with other patterned or textured papers. Even in the simplest rooms, ceilings, windows, and doors, when enhanced by the imaginative use of printed papers and borders, can create grand illusions and make a strong contribution to the room design.

Papered and detailed ceilings

MARBLE-PAPERED CEILING

The extravagant ceiling in the dark and dramatic library below and opposite was created from individually applied 14-inch squares of handmade ruby red Italian marble paper, separated by 3-inch green marble "keys." The curved cove around the outside edges of the ceiling was papered in wide strips of the green marble paper, separated from the red center by a 3-inch sienna brown "stripe." Each of the individual elements was then outlined with permanent markers in overlapping strokes of Van Dyke brown over bright gold. Finally, the entire ceiling was sealed with two coats of polyurethane.

Most of us have learned to live with plain-Jane ceilings—boring expanses of Sheetrock and sterile swaths of off-white paint. It's only in the last seventy-five years, however, that ceilings have been virtually unadorned and ignored. The intricate plaster or wood details of ornate ceilings, for centuries an integral part of residential design, are too hard on today's budgets. And even if we chose to invest, carvers and artisans are increasingly a vanishing breed. Papers, however, can offer a broad variety of looks at a wide range of prices. There are wallpapers printed to resemble Gothic fretwork, lattice, elaborate coffering, stone and marble inlay. All are very effective when applied overhead. Some papers look like blue sky with clouds and can turn a bleak room into a garden. There are hundreds of small-scale nondirectional prints, textural, geometric, and floral, that can be hung successfully on ceilings to add liveliness, color, and pattern to the room. The one drawback to papered ceilings is that the seams may be visible. This is an issue that has never bothered us much, adding, we believe, to the hand-crafted look of the room. The decora-

GILT-PAPERED CEILING

When we first saw the room below, the plaster upper-wall and ceiling moldings were nearly invisible because they had been painted off-white to match the walls and ceiling. We had them repainted in mahogany brown to duplicate the restored wood trim throughout the apartment, and then we papered the ceiling in gold-leaf wallpaper. Our client was thrilled at how the gilt ceiling glowed in the reflected light.

CELESTIAL CEILING

This ceiling is a good example of the successful use of a modestly scaled all-over pattern, which, because of the metallic stars and the richness of the background color, adds a striking and dramatic note to the room's quiet, neutral color scheme. The use of elaborate borders, applied both to the actual ceiling and to the curved cove molding we cemented along the ceiling line, gives the whole room a little lift, creating the illusion that the ceiling, just 9 feet high, is slightly vaulted. The real magic comes from the subtle glow produced by waxing and buffing the papered ceiling. Yes, it's hard work to wax and buff over your head, but the finished ceiling is really superb!

BORDERED BATHROOM

We loved the look of this border against the subtle strié wallpaper, but as hard as we tried, we couldn't find a way to use it successfully on the walls because of some awkward soffits and changes of ceiling level. By continuing the strié paper up and over the soffit, however, we emphasized this nearly perfect little ceiling. So, up went the border . . . overhead, where it adds a quiet charm.

LEAF ROOM CEILING,
PREVIOUS PAGE

Since there was no ceiling line, there was no logical place to stop the paper on the garret wall in this little room. By continuing this spectacular pressed-leaf paper up and onto the ceiling, we created the illusion of height and turned a negative into a positive. The ceiling "border" was cut from long strips of paper trimmed with great variation around individual leaves, continuing the feeling of a partial leafy roof overhead, and small clusters and individual leaves were applied here and there on the ceiling, rounding the corners slightly.

tive boost papers offer can far outweigh the nuisance of seam lines.

One of the most obvious ways to integrate the ceiling into the overall room design is to cover it in the same paper as the walls. This will work successfully only if the paper is nondirectional (that is, with no obvious top and bottom to the pattern) and not too dark, heavy, or otherwise visually demanding, and if the height of the ceiling can handle the addition of pattern and color. Bathrooms with no crown moldings, particularly those that are half tiled, can be enhanced by running the paper up and over the ceiling. In rooms with garret ceilings that flow right down into one or two of the walls, continuing the paper onto the ceiling eases the awkwardness. In tiny rooms, using the same paper throughout can create an intimate quality and, in fact, visually enlarge the space. The most extravagant pairing of ceiling and walls is the creation of a gazebo room or a "tent" room where striped walls and sectioned, mitered stripes overhead replicate the inside of a tent.

More often than not, however, using the same paper on the ceiling as on the walls is not an option. If that is the case, consider small prints and light-colored textures. Simply painting the ceiling is often not the best choice, and the nuance of a small pattern or texture overhead can add immeasurably to the integrity of the design.

If your ceilings are very low, if the thought of papering the whole ceiling makes you claustrophobic, or if you simply hate visible seams, you might consider applying a border both to the walls and to the ceiling, or to the ceiling alone. In some cases where beams, soffits, or awkward zigs and zags make borders difficult to use continuously and neatly on the walls, applying them to

ceilings might be the best and most attractive way to introduce them into your design scheme. In many cases, using a border as an extension of the walls can cause the ceiling to appear higher than it actually is and add to the sense of airiness in a room.

If your taste runs to the extraordinary and dramatic and your room height is over 8 feet, the ceiling can provide an extravagant venue for marbled or book papers, bolder or darker patterns like richly colored paisleys, papers that are printed to look like wood, marble, or stone paneling, or silver- or gold-leafed papers. Leafed papers are great favorites of ours. Unfortunately, they are not inexpensive. The papers, which require costly metal leaf and handwork to produce, can cost well over $100 a roll, and since they are not porous and highlight every bump and imperfection on the wall underneath, they nearly always require an experienced professional to install. Cost and installation concerns notwithstanding, leafed papers on the ceiling are gorgeous, totally change the quality of light in a space, and make all of the other colors in the room dance.

DETAILED SUNROOM DOOR
These doors dated back to the 30s, when doors were still doors and therefore had some detail we could work with. This trompe l'oeil stone pattern in a brick design, framed with scraps of unused border from the paneled walls, added just enough drama and pattern.

PAPER-PANELED DOORS
Here we achieved a tongue-in-cheek version of elegantly paneled doors by papering the inexpensive hollow-core doors that open into this living room with two softly textured papers and an architectural border.

Papered and detailed windows and doors

Don't make the mistake of thinking papers are for walls alone; doors and windows, too, can benefit from the addition of paper elements.

Doors offer unusual decorating opportunities. Panel doors can be trimmed with borders used alone over paint or in combination with other patterned papers or interesting textures. Even lowly hollow-core doors, a builder's favored cost-cutter and residential eyesore, can be immeasurably enhanced

BORDERED WINDOW FRAMES
Windows with flat frames like these, above, offer a wonderful space for the application of a narrow border. This vine was cut free from the ground paper and applied as if it were growing around the windows. For bay windows with shutters, paper can provide a touch of pattern and color while avoiding the awkward installation of individual curtains.

with papers and borders. Textures layered with architectural borders can turn this liability into an aesthetic asset.

Years ago, we began to work with a client who detested fabric window treatments, having been subjected in childhood, we suspect, to some drapery atrocities. It was a struggle for us, loving fabrics as we do, to find ways to keep her windows from becoming big empty spaces in the walls. To her everlasting credit, Susan, our client, taught us that windows can be beautiful without a single yard of fabric.

Later in our career we began what has become an ongoing romance with the use of applied papers to decorate window openings. Although they cannot provide protection from sunlight or afford privacy as curtains do, engineered papers and borders can bring color and pattern to windows. They can, of course, be used in combination with fabric window treatments, but the beauty of borders for windows where room-darkening or privacy is not a prime issue is that they bring style to the room for a fraction of the cost. Borders can run happily around flat frames, jazzing them up without interfering with the view beyond. This idea can also be used to make small windows more important in a room or, if the border has an architectural look, to bring a more substantial structural detail to an unimpressive opening. You might even create window frames from architecturally printed border papers in situations where the architect or builder cut corners and left you with little if any wood trim.

The way you choose to cut out your borders will greatly influence the look of the finished window. If you are working with a viny border printed on a ground paper of a different color than the trim or wall, cutting it out com-

DRAMATIC DOOR

In this strange and wonderful little library using a grape leaf border around the windows and door was a way to reiterate the pattern-against-pattern theme. The border appears on the ceiling as well, but its use along the flat window trims and door frames puts it smack dab in front of the eye. Since the border doesn't quite match the wallcovering, it was crucial to use it very deliberately—too little and it looks like an afterthought. The door here is particularly successful because it combines the grape leaf border with a bold tortoiseshell texture . . . all of which becomes very three-dimensional and exciting in the room.

FLORAL SUNROOM

In this charming sunroom we combined blossoms cut individually and in groups from an all-over floral print with this bamboo fretwork sidewall's companion border to create our own gloriously flowered border design, repeated in 48-inch lengths. More flowers bloom above the window and in the center of the two diamond window panes.

FRAMED WINDOW WITH SHUTTERS

If you love the look of country house windows framed with trailing English ivy, here is a maintenance-free version. An ivy border was carefully scissor-cut along one side; the mismatched mitered corners had to be "disguised" by the addition of individual leaves. An assembled cluster of ivy details the shutters.

pletely from the ground paper before applying it to the frame enhances the illusion that it's actually growing along the window edge. Freeing the border in this way allows it to float on the trim or wall color and makes it look three-dimensional. If you choose a border with the same ground color as the frame or wall (white, for example), you can save a great deal of cutting time by leaving one straight edge and simply butting it up against the window frame. The technical and aesthetic choices you must make here are similar to the choices you make when applying borders on walls along the ceiling line.

Wood cornices can be papered, as can shutters and shades. One of the most successful window treatments we've ever designed was a shaped wood cornice on which we applied a wide variety of paper elements, all of which related to the fabric and border used in the room but none of which exactly duplicated them. In this way, we were

able to add immeasurably to the complexity of the room design without overwhelming it. Since everything was cut out and glued on the cornices, piece by piece, we had nearly total design freedom, something not even the huge and diverse fabric market can offer. This technique also works well on paneled wood shutters where the small blank spaces can be turned into "framed" works of applied paper art.

Of course, paper can always be used on window shades. The most interesting way to do this is to create a border on the shade, using a printed border or one you assemble yourself from cut elements. By keeping the work narrow and placing it horizontally along the bottom edge of the shade, you will not interfere with the roller operation and can still raise or lower the shade to the top of the applied border. If you want to completely cover a shade, there are companies that specialize in laminating wallpapers to shades. Depending upon the final surface finish, you might then add your own cut paper details over the wallpapered shade, being careful to use thin papers so that the shade doesn't get too bulky.

Finally, you might consider découpaging birds, flowers, or other small elements right on a windowpane, an interesting way to add detail to the room while altering or disguising the view a bit. This is an idea that works best in climates where there aren't extremes in temperature, but if you're willing to accept the possibility of some peeling due to moisture or cold, it's an effective way to expand your decorating scheme.

Ceilings, windows, and doors—all of these architectural elements offer you the possibility of extending your decorating scheme beyond traditional confines and into fresh and exciting new territory.

DECORATIVE ROLLER SHADES
These very ordinary but practical off-white window shades became an attractive part of the kitchen design scheme when brightly colored fruit was added along the bottom edges. The fruit was cut from an all-over fruit-printed wallpaper and artfully placed low enough to allow the shades to be raised and lowered. The fruit motif is repeated in the trompe l'oeil armoire panels and in a more delicate way on the checkerboard wallpaper. Notice how a diagonal strip of that checkerboard was run around the room to finish off the wall at the ceiling line, an effective visual divider when there is no wood crown molding.

Detailed Ceilings, Windows, and Doors **81**

CREATING PAPER-DECORATED PLYWOOD CORNICES

Paper-covered and -decorated plywood cornices can carry the color and pattern of a border or wallpapered walls across the top of a window opening without the expense of fabric window treatments, or decorate a window without fuss. Here are some helpful guidelines:

- Unless your window span is very large, ½-inch birch plywood should work for your cornice. For smaller than normal windows, ⅜-inch plywood may be all you need.

- Design your cornice as you would a fabric valance; a good rule of thumb is to keep the body of the cornice confined to the upper one-fifth of the window opening. Side drops should not fall below the top one-third.

- Build the cornice with a face, two sides (or returns), and a full top. With a top you can install the cornice easily with angle irons, which, because they will be inside the cornice and high overhead, will be invisible. If the cornice is planned to go over fabric side panels, make the sides, or returns, of the cornice deep enough to accommodate the fabric panels when they are fully open; we generally allow 8–9 inches.

- After the cornice is cut to the desired shape, paint the outside and the bottom edges with a coat of primer and apply a sizing to strengthen the bond of the paper to the wood. Prime and paint the inside in a color close to the ground color of the background paper.

- Try to select a background paper that you can railroad, or run horizontally across the cornice, thus avoiding vertical seams.

- Cover the cornice with the railroaded background paper, wrapping it across the long front of the cornice, around the outside edges, over the sides (or returns), and onto the back of the sides.

- If you are repeating a border used around the ceiling line across the top of your cornice, you are not obliged to use it exactly the same way. Try cutting into the bottom of the border along the cornice, for example, to soften the way the border meets the background paper. This will also eliminate the disruption of a straight line through the body of the cornice, a plus if your cornice is shaped in some way. The border *must* center attractively on the cornice, even if this means that it does not match perfectly where it joins the walls. Since the cornice protrudes into the room, any differences in the placement of the repeats will hardly be noticeable.

- You can use almost any paper element to decorate a cornice. Scraps of borders, appliqués, paper napkins, doilies, shelf edging, color copies, prints, gift cards . . . use your imagination. Start with the main and secondary elements, and then fill in with the smaller elements. See pages 193 and 207 for information on adhesives.

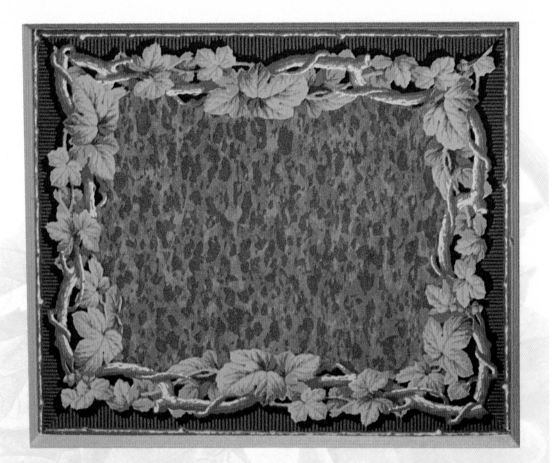

DISGUISING UNMATCHED MITERS

A border with flowers, leaves, or other such busy patterns is often difficult to miter attractively. This is because the straight lines along the diagonal cuts will be very obvious in a pattern with small, busy, curved shapes. In many cases, no matter how hard you try, the miters will be mismatched. If you have this problem, here are some tips to help disguise these miters:

▪ Cut the miter as you normally would, lining up any printed outside pattern lines or, if none exist, the cut outside edges. You might find it easier to cut one piece at a time, using the first cut angle as a guide to cut the second. In that way you can slip the second strip around a bit to find the best place. If there

are no main elements to deal with, this becomes a matter of personal preference. No matter where you place the miter, it will look mismatched and remain visible in borders of this kind because it is the only straight line cutting through the pattern.

▪ Glue the miter in place. Now, find elements in the scraps that you can isolate, cut out, and apply in several places over the miter to disguise the mismatch and the straight diagonal line. It might be a leaf, a group of leaves, or an individual blossom. Either use something that will disappear or pick a strong element that you can isolate on the corners, turning the problem into a positive design statement.

PART 2

PAPERED AND EMBELLISHED FURNITURE AND ACCESSORIES

In interior design and decoration, as in the old song, little things mean a lot. Through the addition of paper-embellished furniture, a découpaged tray that replicates your antique prints, a collection of beautifully papered boxes, mirrors that reflect your good taste, or an evocative memorabilia screen, your handiwork can enhance your home, add a touch of humor or glamour, and bring it to life.

In this section we pay homage to traditional découpage in objects both old and new, and also offer you our own versions and adaptations, designed to have maximum impact with minimum fuss. And it is here that we highlight papers that come by the sheet rather than by the roll. We pull out the bags and boxes of odds and ends, favorites from the clipping files and the print bins at the secondhand store. Handmade papers, old love letters, gift cards from the attic. Bits and pieces that can become the basis of brilliant little accessories. Here are a few of our favorite things.

Decorated Screens, Firescreens, and Fireboards

Screens are ideal playgrounds for cut papers. Not only do they

satisfy a multitude of design needs, they offer a perfectly manageable

blank space: large enough to do something creative with

room-scale impact, but small enough to complete easily. Papered and

paper-decorated screens can be used to divide spaces within a large

This exquisite screen was made with hand-printed panels from one of the oldest and finest wallpaper companies in the world, Zuber & Cie, France. Founded in 1797 at the time of the French Revolution, Zuber has become synonymous with extravagantly conceived, fabulously detailed papers, panels, and borders. This panel paper comes with the gilt border printed right into the pattern and, like all panel prints, requires that the screen be cut to fit the panel rather than the other way around.

Folding screens and room dividers

MINIATURE SCREEN

This Lilliputian tabletop screen is the handiwork of interior designer Michael Zabriski. It was fastidiously constructed, using architect's pine for the framework and a heavy-weight drawing paper for the panel fronts. Michael painted eighteenth-century Chinese motifs in gouaches on the front panels and découpaged small cutouts of flowers and a birdcage on bits of French wallpapers on the back. The screen is magical and, incredibly, not a hair over 6 inches tall!

room, either as tall and elegant partial "walls" or cut shorter to allow the eye to look over and beyond them. They can serve as a backdrop for a sofa, a group of chairs, a table, or other furniture you want to highlight in the room. They can give scale to a room, adding needed height and visual weight in a room of low or smaller-scale furnishings much in the way bookcases and armoires do but for far less money. Screens can fill dull corners with pattern and color, and executed on a smaller scale, they can become attractive tabletop accessories. They can be hung on the wall as art. Antique screens, of course, are very collectible. Some of the most interesting, called memorabilia screens, are those made in nineteenth-century England from hundreds of cutouts, gift cards, and souvenirs—a sort of room-sized scrapbook. They represent a very personal kind of découpage. Small screens and fireboards can decorate firebox openings when they are not in use, turning those little black holes in the wall into beautifully decorated spaces.

From a design point of view, screens are really hinged art. They can be very simple, adding a bit of pattern and color to a room, or as complex as you choose, incorporating multiple papers, borders, cut-out motifs, bits and pieces of memorabilia, or cut-out fruits, flowers, animals . . . your imagination is the only limit. You can even use a plywood-based wallpapered screen as a background against which you display framed art, designing the screen to enhance the pictures, which are simply hung from hooks hammered into the

PRINT SCREEN WITH CLASSICAL HEADS

Beautiful original prints were applied to this dramatic black-and-gold print screen in the early nineteenth century. The prints are a series; that is, they were produced in a numbered sequence and constitute a full collection. Heads of emperors and empresses mix with classical tableaux, floating like exquisite sculpted plaques on the black lacquer ground.

wood. And screens can be decorated on one or both sides, allowing you, like Lord Byron (whose dual passions were boxing and theater, one represented on each side of his famous découpaged room screen), to devote a side to each of two interests or styles. In any case, a beautiful screen covered with things you love will brighten a dark corner, hide the ironing board, accessorize an empty table, and, in short, bring a lovely decorative element into your design schemes.

Because most of the screens we will be discussing here are covered completely with paper, they can be constructed of the simplest and least costly materials; the only constraint is that the surface must be smooth. Nearly all of the screens we've made for this book were built from plywood. Even though panels cut to size from ½-inch plywood will work, heavier ¾-inch panels are less likely to warp. One way to manage cumbersome screens is to construct them in two sections, eliminating some of the hinges, as we did on page 92. You can also use thinner ply by building a frame from 2 × 2's and nailing the lightweight plywood onto the frame. These pieces are less cumbersome to move around but require more carpentry skill. Screens can also be constructed from lightweight, inexpensive hollow-core doors, which are commercially available from lumberyards. If you are working with a handyman or carpenter or have good skills yourself, you can cut these doors to size, finish the cut edge with a narrow piece of wood, prep, paper, and hinge. Screens can also be made from canvas stretchers with lightweight fabric or artist's canvas stretched over and then decorated with applied papers.

Hinges are a multiple-choice issue. There are hinges made especially for

screens, which will bend either direction, allowing you to fold your screen in several ways. A small door hinge will work, although it requires that you predetermine how you want the screen to fold and is more visible when finished. And there are long continuous hinges, called piano hinges, which are as beautiful as they are functional and add a long thin line of shine (either chrome or brass) down each fold. Piano hinges come standard in 4-foot lengths. You can, of course, apply two or more of them contiguously, cutting off any excess with a metal saw. If you want to use them on taller screens without a visible break, you have no choice but to

CORRUGATED SCREEN

We designed this plywood and cardboard screen to have a low, architectural silhouette, and then put it on casters to add to the dressed-down, industrial look. Since corrugated paper marks easily, we had to work carefully while tracing and cutting the panels so as not to flatten the ridges and we used a hot-glue gun to attach the papers since we were unable to roll or smooth it. Turning the cardboard halves of the small appliquéd details on the horizontal or crosswise grain of the paper added dimensionality and a simple, but very effective, pattern.

ART SCREEN

We asked artist Ralph Caparulo to create this low translucent screen for a beach house with expansive windows and beautiful light. The screen was designed to be tall enough to provide the living room with some privacy from the beach, but low enough to not interfere with the sunlight and the view of the ocean beyond. Using wooden canvas stretchers, Ralph stretched sheer but sturdy linen as a background and applied textured rice papers, torn bits of rough, fibrous packing papers, and Chinese "prayer" papers. The finished six-part screen changes from nearly transparent to translucent to opaque with the movement of the sun and is, quite literally, a work of art.

FALLING LEAVES SCREEN

Rather than framing each panel individually, the mitered border of this dramatic screen frames the entire screen, thereby leaving a blank center area across which we glued a shower of "leaves" cut from a second paper. To finish the edges and add a little shine to these dark papers, we mounted each of the cut-out leaves to a piece of Japanese metallic gold paper, cut to the shape of the leaf but larger by $1/4$ inch.

ARCHIMBOLDO TABLE SCREEN

We designed this table screen around sixteenth-century Italian trompe l'oeil artist Archimboldo's cycle of the seasons, cutting color prints of the four faces of summer, winter, autumn, and spring from an exhibition catalog. To add importance to the portraits, we framed them, using two magazine photographs of heavy gilt frames, one rectangular, one round, which were reproduced on a color copier to the correct size. Resting as it does on a sofa table, it is near enough to be enjoyed close up in all its "Archimboldesque" complexity while it cleverly blocks the view of an unattractive apartment building across the street.

GILT SCREEN

This lovely little screen was lying in the corner of a junk shop, covered with old rugs, when the gleam of the gold tea-leaf paper caught Donna's eye. It was constructed of very thin plywood glued onto a wood frame, and the front, back, and edges of each panel were papered. It was a true find!

JAPANESE FAN SCREEN

An extraordinary nineteenth-century Japanese fan screen, made of six panels covered in soft, silvery-gold tea-leaf paper and decorated with flattened paper fans, dominates a long living room wall. The screen could, of course, stand on the floor, but we chose to hang it flat so that each unique panel could be seen and appreciated. Even though this example is old and very valuable, the design itself is simple, direct, and could easily be translated into a contemporary piece.

order them custom-sized, a costly alternative.

As with all interior furnishings, you must consider the size of your room and the height of the ceiling before deciding on the size of a screen. The trick is to balance the width of the panels with their height and with the total width of all the panels after they have been hinged together. There are no hard rules about the proper proportions for a screen. Some are designed to be rather short and squat; others to be tall and elegant. The pattern of the paper or papers you plan to apply to the screen will, in some instances, control the width and height of the panels. For example, if you are using a panel-printed paper, you will have to deal with the printed width of the pattern and, unless you are adding a border, cut your wood panel width to match. Allowing for the best placement of other less obvious patterns is always a good idea. Even a small lattice should fall in a way that is the most attractive, with the edges lining up with a logical place on the lattice pattern, both at the sides and at the top and bottom. Some screens, therefore, will need to be custom-cut in order to perfectly accommodate the paper. Evaluate your paper choices before deciding on the size of the panels.

Screens can be designed in sections or as one unit that incorporates all of the separate panels in an overall design. The same six-panel screen could be planned as six separate areas; each panel could be divided into two or three sections, stacked one over the other, creating twelve or eighteen separate areas; or all six panels could be united by a border run around the outside edges and the interior decorated as if it were one large canvas, disregarding the breaks between the panels. Often the overall design of the room will dictate how

strong or fragmented the design of the screen can be and still contribute to the scheme. Of course there is also the back of the screen panels to consider. Some screens are used free-standing in the middle of a room, with both the back and the front decorated.

An important consideration in screen design is the direction in which the hinges will fold. Unless you are able to locate screen hinges that allow you to bend the panels in either direction, you will have to decide early on if your screen will bend to make an M, a W, or a Z. M and W configurations are screens with an even number of panels; Z's are an uneven number. With M configurations, the two outside panels in the screen come forward into the room. These screens work best in corners, where they will fit snugly, the two outside edges running parallel to the two walls. M's don't take up too much floor space but, consequently, don't provide much storage space behind. W configurations work well for a screen that will simply stand along a wall or in a corner where you want space left behind the screen. As a rule, W's take up more floor space than M's. If you are using prominent hinges like piano hinges, W screens will really display them, with two rows running right down the front. Only one row of hinges is displayed on M screens.

Z configurations work well in corners and have a nice irregular look to them. It is hard, however, to execute a really balanced design on a Z because one end panel will turn toward you and the other will turn away, causing an imbalance in the way you see the design. Whatever you apply to panels that angle sharply, either toward you or away from you, of course, will distort slightly in the eye. Therefore, if your pattern or design requires that it be seen

HERALDIC SCREEN
Because the walls in this room were intricately paneled, hanging art was nearly impossible. Using the screen as a wall, we were able to display these old hand-colored prints of knights in shining armor in frames rather than by gluing them. The sidewall, border, tassels, and fabric swags are from four different papers, all with a heraldic design quality and similar coloring. After we determined the placement of the framed prints, we cut out the decorative appliqués and pasted them onto the screen. Finally, picture hooks were hammered in and the prints were hung.

VICTORIAN SCRAP SCREEN
Hundreds of small cutouts, cards, and photographs were assembled and glued onto this leather Victorian scrap screen more than a hundred years ago. The natural aging of the varnish has given the screen a lovely mellow patina, muting the once riotous colors. You can create this aged look by adding tints of burnt umber or raw sienna to your finishing coat of varnish or polyurethane. The more coats, the deeper the amber glow.

CREATING A WALLPAPERED PLYWOOD SCREEN

Building a screen from plywood is a simple process. The choice of height, width, and number of panels will vary with the amount of available room space, the way you want to use the screen, and the paper or papers you will use to decorate it. Using the guidelines we offer in this chapter, make these decisions, determining the number and size of your individual panels. The thickness of the plywood you use should be based on the size of the screen: ½ inch works well for small screens; ¾ inch is best for screens taller than 4 feet. If you plan to use picture hooks on your screen or to hammer nails into the screen for any reason, ¾ inch is the better choice. You will need to select a folding configuration at this time as well, choosing an M, W, or Z fold for your screen. Finally, select the type of hinges you will use based on the aesthetics of the paper, the direction the screen will fold, and your personal preference. Now you are ready to begin:

1. Based on the size and number of panels, determine the number of sheets of plywood you will need to buy. Plywood comes in 4- × -8-foot sheets. If you can, size the screen panels in the most economical way, getting two panels per sheet of plywood. If you are having the plywood cut to size at a lumberyard, you will pay for every cut. Therefore, if you choose panels 24 inches wide (requiring a single lengthwise cut per sheet), it will cost slightly less than requesting panels 22 inches wide. Purchase the plywood and have it cut to size.

2. If you have ordered birch ply-wood, the surface should be smooth enough for papering. If not, apply several coats of primer to the panels or use gesso to fill in the cracks and smooth the surface. Sand until the surface is smooth and even. Be sure to prepare both sides of the panels and to sand and prime all of the edges.

3. If you are planning to paper the panels completely and to wrap the paper around the edges to the back, you will not need to apply finish coats of paint. Should you wish to leave the edges unpapered or to découpage on a painted screen rather than on paper, paint those surfaces with the background paint color.

4. Apply sizing over the entire surface to help secure the paper and keep it from shrinking.

5. Plan the final placement of the paper, centering it in the most attractive way side to side and top to bottom. Cut strips of paper to fit the width and length of the panels plus 3½ inches. This will allow you to wrap the paper around the edges and approximately 1 inch onto the back at the top, bottom, and sides.

6. Paper the screen with the ground paper, following the instructions included in the roll and using the guidelines for wallpapering in the "Tools, Terms, and Techniques" chapters. At the corners, lift up the excess paper and pinch it together with the edges matching, making little rabbit ears. Following the corner edge, cut off the protruding rabbit ears flush to the plywood. Wrap the remaining paper onto the back, mitering it at the corners.

7. If you are planning to paper the back of the screen, in either matching or contrasting paper, do that now. To cut the back pieces, measure the panel and subtract 1 inch from the height and 1 inch from the width. When it is applied, ½ inch of the face paper will be visible around the outside edges.

8. Hammer plastic glides into the bottom of each panel. These allow you to move the screen more easily after it is assembled and protect your floor from scratches. Glides also protect the paper at the bottom edge of the screen.

9. If you are using a border, apply it with border adhesive, centering the pattern in the most attractive way on the panels and mitering all corners. Clean all excess adhesive away with a clean soft sponge.

10. Finalize the placement of any cut decorative elements on the panels by laying them in place and making any design adjustments. Then glue them in place, one by one, using border adhesive or white glue to ensure the bond. Clean off all excess adhesive thoroughly with a sponge.

11. You can choose to seal the finished screen or not. Consider the end use of the screen, whether it is in a place where it will need to be touched frequently or might be spattered with food or drink. Evaluate the fragility of the paper elements and the amount of pure white in the screen. Any finish, even latex urethane, will yellow slightly after a few years. Varnish will yellow as it is applied. If you choose to seal, follow the guidelines for choosing and using sealants on pages 207–208.

12. Finally, apply the hinges to the panels. Be sure to check and double-check that the hinges are folding in the correct direction before screwing them into place. Screwing into a narrow edge is difficult; this may be a task for a carpenter or, at the very least, a person with some woodworking skill.

This richly colored and intricately patterned fan screen was made from a wallpaper sidewall with an applied border. The color and drama of this paper and border add a perfect touch to the elegant room, bringing summer glamour to the empty firebox opening.

without too much distortion in order to be understood, it is a good idea to plan for a screen that is more open, less folded, and will, therefore, take up more linear floor space. The extreme of this is, of course, applying screens flat on the wall. Hanging valuable antique screens like pictures allows every nuance to be seen and enjoyed without any distortion or shadow at all.

Firescreens and fireboards

DELLA ROBBIA FIREBOARD

The curved top of this fireboard was cut to echo the graceful curves of the carved and gilt swags on the mantel. Elegant green and brown marble papers from Italy, purchased at an art store, were applied to the board. Then laser color copies of some fine nineteenth-century hand-colored fruit and bird prints were applied like a Della Robbia garland, enhancing the somewhat Italianate flavor of the room design.

These special screens add a small but significant touch of color and design to an empty firebox and thereby enhance the room. You can design a paper fan screen from a favorite wallpaper and border, glue a favorite poster onto a piece of custom-cut birch plywood, mix Italian marble papers and ripe and rosy fruit prints for a Della Robbia fireboard, or create a fireboard collage with old newspapers, antique personal papers, and mementos.

Pleated firescreens can be made from almost any wallpaper. Only those that refuse to hold a crease must be eliminated from the contenders. You will need to consider the pattern on your paper when you determine the width of the folds, but 1½ inches works very well and should be the ideal. If you choose to add a border to the fan screen, choose a pattern that will relate attractively when folded.

The key to a successful fireboard project is to use birch plywood as a base, since it provides the smoothest surface. Either ½-inch or ¾-inch thickness will do; the choice depends on personal preference. The heavier plywood is less likely to warp but more difficult to move around. The "stand" can be custom-cut from two separate pieces of wood, or made by routing out

REVERSIBLE FIREBOARD

Artist Ralph Caparulo's artful fireboard is covered entirely, front and back, with bits of old newspaper, letters, and old prints. The artist has worked into some of them, scribbling with a charcoal pencil. The papers were glued to the plywood with artist's matte medium, which was painted on the back with a soft-bristle brush and then painted over the finished collage as a sealant.

a narrow trough in a door saddle that has been cut to the appropriate length.

We always design fireboards individually to complement the room for which they are intended. Repeating the basic shape of the firebox opening is one approach, of course, but you can also custom-cut the board to follow the shape of any design you choose. These jigsaw patterns require some fancy carpentry but are charming in a simple fireplace. In most cases, you will want to paint the raw wood a dark, low-luster color so that the plywood edge disappears in the darkness of the firebox. If you are using wood other than birch, you may need to gesso the face of your fireboard to fill in the grain lines and create a smoother surface before applying the paper motifs.

Finishing a screen or fireboard

FLORAL FIREBOARD

The shape of this plywood fireboard was cut to follow the shape of poster art. Using tracing paper, we copied the bouquet's shape for the carpenter to jigsaw. We painted the edge of the cut ply black to cause it to blend in with the firebox. Once the poster was glued to the board with heavy-duty vinyl adhesive, the edges were carefully cut back with a craft knife. Finally, we used a black marker to touch up the cut edges of the poster.

Both room screens and firescreens and -boards can be sealed. All of the antique screens featured here were carefully sealed with varnish. We did not, however, seal any of our screens. None would be subjected to wear and tear, and we did not want to risk having any of the papers yellow over the years. We did, however, seal our fireboards. Sealing fireboards is a process similar to sealing most découpage. You may choose not to seal at all, but if soil would be visible, you will need to apply a protective topcoat. In all cases but one, we used polyurethane to seal. The exception was our newspaper and memento fireboard, which was sealed with an extra coat of the same material used as the adhesive, artist's matte medium, a material available at art supply stores. In any case, no fireboard or fan screen made of paper can be left in place once a fire is lit.

MAKING A FAN FIRESCREEN

Folded paper fan screens can be made from almost any commercially available wallpaper; the only requirement is that it can be crisply folded to create the accordion pleating. Adding a border is, of course, optional, but edging the screen with a border provides an attractive finishing touch. Follow these easy steps to create a fan firescreen of your own:

1. Cut a 2-yard length of wallpaper for the body of your fan. If you are using a border paper, cut a 2-yard length, allowing a bit extra if the pattern needs to be centered on the fan.

2. Virtually any of the standard wallpaper widths are fine for this project. Compare the width of your paper with the width of your firebox. If the width of your firebox opening is twice the width of your paper, that is an ideal proportion. If you have chosen a very wide paper, you may need to trim it down.

3. Place the border on the paper and adjust the pattern to the most attractive placement. Glue the border to the paper using border adhesive. Clean off all excess glue with a soft clean sponge.

4. To make the folds, use a pencil to mark along both edges on the back of the paper at 1¼-inch intervals. You should have 59 lines, which will give you 29 folds on the face of the finished screen. Starting from the back of the paper, use a straightedge to line up the marks and accordion-pleat the length of paper. To set the folds, use a nonscratching tool like a smoother or your fingernail and go over each

fold, pressing it until it is crisp and sharp.

5. The first and last folds will hold the weights, which enable the screen to stand. To make a pocket into which you will glue the weights, both of the outside folds must turn back. Shorten one side if

necessary to make these folds match. Glue a weight, 1 × 6 inches, onto the back of the two outside folds, 1 inch down from the top of the screen. Two 6-inch metal rules from a stationer or 1-inch square drapery weights placed end to end serve the same purpose and are easy to find. Finish gluing the entire length of the fold.

6. Holding the folded screen tightly at the bottom, wrap around the bottom edge with a 4-inch length of ⅞-inch-wide coordinating grosgrain ribbon. Glue the ribbon in place.

7. You can finish the screen with a 1½-inch decorative metal rosette with a screw through the center hole. Push the rosette screw straight through the grosgrain ribbon and into the folds of the fan.

Elaborated Tables and Other Furniture

Historically, the classic art of découpage as we know it,

from its beginnings in the seventeenth century until the present, has

included fine and beautiful work on furniture as well as screens

and small objects such as boxes, lamps, and trays. In Venice in the

seventeenth and eighteenth centuries, découpage was called

"l'arte del uòmo pòvero," literally "poor man's art," because it provided

a way for the less wealthy to acquire colorful decorated furniture

without incurring the expense of painted or lacquered pieces from China or Japan. Découpage was practiced with great success by English furniture makers as well as the French and Germans during the eighteenth century. Detailing furniture with cut papers, therefore, comes to us with a long and cherished heritage.

It also comes with a reputation for requiring arduous, highly skilled labor. Mary Havlicek, the remarkably able and patient woman with whom we worked on many of the projects in this book, studied découpage with a master from the traditional school. Her projects over the years, all done in the classic manner, took months to complete. We set out at a pace that startled her, accustomed as she was to the tediously slow and methodical classic procedure. Our master plan, however, was to find ways to accomplish the *look* without turning each project into a mission . . . in brief, to eliminate most of the frustrating time and effort. No one wants to tackle a project in July with few prospects of finishing by Christmas. Therefore, although we show a number of very traditional and complex projects made by others, all of the tables and furniture we made for this chapter are done with a looser, more forgiving technique. We've kept the chore of cutting with manicuring scissors, for example, to a minimum by choosing bolder prints or a bolder cutting of prints. Wherever possible we've chosen to seal the furniture with just a few coats of latex urethane, which dries crystal clear and fast and allows for soap and water cleanup. Some of the pieces have been carefully waxed. Others have not. Some of the tables could easily be lightly sealed and then protected by glass tops, thereby eliminating multiple coats of sealant altogether. Keeping the

PIETRA DURA TOP, ABOVE, AND PAGE 105

Using leftover wallpapers and laser copies of old fruit prints, we designed this tabletop to resemble extremely costly and heavy pietra dura, inlaid stone and marble slabs. The octagonal tabletop was cut from ³/₄-inch birch plywood with a 2-inch-wide wood band applied around the outside edge to give it the appearance of a thicker material. The top was sealed with latex polyurethane, which dries clear, preserving the pale colors.

HIRAM MANNING MASTERPIECE

This exquisite Venetian bombe commode was masterfully découpaged by Hiram Manning in the eighteenth-century style, colored with costly madder red paint and a group of hand-colored eighteenth-century prints and decorative elements. Notice the attention paid to the placement of the individual cuttings and border elements. Even the negative spaces between cartouches are designed to be an appealing shape and size.

Jered Holmes created these whimsical nesting tables using auction catalogs and magazine clippings of chairs, sofas, tables, and accessories. The découpaged sections are covered by practical glass, which fits down into the wood-bordered tops.

constraints of end use in mind, you can freely choose the level of finishing, from very little for a decorative piece that will get no real wear to multiple layers of sealant for a cocktail table. In any case, we urge you not to let the technical demands of the craft stop you from enjoying the aesthetic rewards.

Tables and tabletops

ANIMAL TABLE

A tribute to traditional découpage style, this cocktail table, designed and executed by Mary Havlicek and photographed in a room designed by Anthony Antine, features a menagerie of animals cut from old prints. The tabletop is Formica laminate, which afforded Mary a perfect surface on which to attach the delicately trimmed pieces. This work is not for the impatient or unskilled, of course, but even though it took considerable time to do and many coats of varnish to finish, the process was the same as simpler work. The table has been used by Mary and her family for many years and has become a very personal family heirloom.

Tabletops are the simplest of furniture pieces to découpage and are a natural for cut-paper projects of many different styles and levels of complexity. You can recycle a shabby old table by first sanding it carefully and prep-coating it with a good-quality primer, and then embellishing it with découpage. You can have an inexpensive new top cut for an old base by a carpenter or lumberyard and then turn plain plywood into a princely showpiece. New, affordable, but boring tables can be given an instant heritage with papers. Even lowly self-adhesive papers can be used to transform the ordinary into the unusual.

All tabletops offer a simple flat surface on which to build interesting designs. The tables featured here run the gamut from the quick to the complex. The skill requirements of the ones that feature faux-finish stone or textured papers designed to look like intricately cut and inlaid stonework pietra dura tops, for example, have more to do with measuring, planning, and accurately cutting your design than with the task of meticulously freeing tiny, complex flowers and the like from prints. If you have a good head for measuring, a table like the *pietra dura* octagon would be fun. On the other hand, if tiny, intricate work interests you, the more classically styled animal cocktail table might be your perfect winter project.

DÉCOUPAGED END TABLES

Libby Cameron, an interior designer and découpeure, lives with her young family in a spacious sun-filled loft that's chock full of Libby's découpaged pieces. The little bumper end table, below, *and cottage-style bedside piece,* above, *(now in the collection of Mr. and Mrs. Cully Irving) are perfect examples of Libby's unstudied style. On one, birds and animals frolic around on the top and shelf without a hint of elaborate design plotting. On the other, bouquets are tossed about in ingenuous disregard for fussy balancing. Pieces like these are a wonderful foil to more involved designs and offer another view of decorated furniture for those of us for whom personalized furniture should be fun to look at as well as fun to do.*

Whether your table is old or new, its shape, both the top and the base, will often influence the choice of design elements and the way they are applied. One example of this is the small black lacquer and Formica cocktail table onto which we applied a "leopard skin" paper and "nailheads." The shape of the tabletop suggested an animal skin; it was a perfect place to use this trompe l'oeil paper. Round tabletops are extremely versatile, inviting both strictly geometric sectioning and loose, wreath-like garlands of flowers, fruit, or other small elements. Borders work best on squares, rectangles, octagons, and the like; you can, however, border a round or oval table if you select a narrow border that allows you to slash into the pattern every ½ inch or so, and then slightly overlap the sections so that the straight border will turn around the curved sides.

If a tabletop has serious damages or other liabilities that make working on it too difficult, or if you have a base without a top, don't hesitate to have a new top cut from ¾-inch birch plywood. A plywood top can be primed and sanded to provide an excellent surface for découpage. The outside edge can be finished with a strip of brass gallery rail (available at specialty hardware stores) or with a 2-inch, L-shaped, thin wood strip applied around the edge with tiny finishing nails. Most of the new tops we used in the work made for this book were cut from plywood and finished with such strips, provided and applied by a lumberyard. After the strips are painted with several coats of paint, the découpage is cut and applied, and the whole thing is sealed and waxed, you would never suspect that the tabletop was made of homely plywood.

It is always a good idea to paint the surface of the tabletop with either a color-matched or a strongly contrasting background color. Then, if a corner isn't completely covered or you are papering the edges separately from the top, the thin lines left uncovered will blend into your design or, if you use a contrasting color, outline the papered areas. Over the painted surface, you might choose to apply gold or silver leaf, either over the entire surface or to specific areas according to your design. Available through art supply stores, leaf comes in little sheets, put together in "books" of twenty-five, and is applied one sheet at a time over a painted prep coat and a second coat of a special colorless sizing. The sizing is painted on, and when it has dried to the right degree of tackiness, the leaf is gently placed over it, tapped into place with a soft brush, and burnished with a cloth. Real gold or silver leaf costs a fortune; metal leaf, called Dutch leaf, is perfectly acceptable for most projects, particularly projects where only a tiny bit shows. Dutch leaf is made from gold- and silver-colored aluminum and costs one-fifth as much as real gold or silver leaf. And while metal leaf may tarnish and turn slightly green over a long period of time, we rarely use real gold or silver leaf where it is a tiny part of the design, reserving that kind of investment for embellishing good frames or objects of great value.

If you are creating a tabletop with the look of inlaid stone or marble, you should not apply the different papers in layers, one glued over the other, since layering will leave exposed edges that are visible and difficult to bury in coats of sealant. This may not be a problem on a wall or ceiling, but it will affect the quality of your work on a tabletop, which is viewed close up. The best way is to "float" the papers on a layer of gold or silver leaf or on a dark painted back-

TRAY TABLES

TV tables are a ubiquitous and, generally, unsightly addition to most households. Here a "woodgrain" folding table was given a classy new look with a color copy of the owner's antique horse print and a stylish checkerboard wallpaper border.

LEOPARD-SKIN COCKTAIL TABLE

When spotted at a secondhand store and sporting a chipped cherry wood laminate top, this elegant table had nothing in its favor but its pleasing shape and graceful proportions. However, after the application of some wood filler, two coats of black lacquer, and a wallpaper leopard skin outlined with "nailheads" hole-punched from a border, it is as chic as they come.

MERCURY GLASS/DÉCOUPAGE COCKTAIL TABLE

This table, covered with a piece of old venetian mercury glass, has a border of old prints sandwiched between the wood top and the mottled silvery glass. The table, made during the early years of this century, has an old and worn appearance, a look that always adds something warm and genuine to a room scheme.

CHECKERBOARD CUBE TABLE

A vintage 60s table, stored in an attic for decades, made a perfect base for this delightfully drawn checkerboard wallpaper in a pattern called "Hover" designed by artist Carolyn Ray. Because this table is seen from all sides, deciding how to apply the paper in order to minimize the visible cut edges took some thought. The most sensible way to cover it was the top first, the sides next, and the bottom last, even though there would be cut edges visible along the top edges and along the curved bottom. To disguise them, after they were cut out but before the adhesive was applied, we darkened the white edges with a brown marking pen along the brown checks and an ocher pen along the ocher checks.

BEACHCOMBER'S TABLE

We had a carpenter cut a new round top for this rope-wrapped Victorian table and painted the base a fresh, bright turquoise blue with coral paint to detail some of the roping. We covered the new primed top with an allover stipple-textured paper with the look of sand and the color of a Caribbean sea, and arranged copies of wonderful old shell prints in a scattershot style on top. The outer edge of the new top was detailed with part of a rope border paper which "says hello" to the rope-decorated base.

FAUX MARBLE/TOP TABLE

Using leftover wallpapers, we designed the tabletop to resemble extremely costly and heavy pietra dura, inlaid stone and marble slabs. The octagonal tabletop was cut from ³/₄-inch birch plywood with a 2-inch-wide wood band applied around the outside edge to give it the appearance of a thicker material. The top was sealed with latex polyurethane, which dries clear, preserving the pale colors, and which buries the cut edges quickly.

Elaborated Tables and Other Furniture **113**

IMITATING INLAY WITH CUT PAPER

Among the most interesting and challenging of papering projects is the creation of elaborate "inlaid" tops for tables and other furniture. This process requires a great deal of planning, but the cutting and gluing are rather straightforward. To complete these projects successfully, you need a good head for puzzle solving and an inventive eye. Photographs of fine old wood marquetry or marble and stone inlaid tables (called *pietra dura*) can help you conceptualize a design. Our table was designed as a circle that was divided into 6 equal sections, each outlined by ¼-inch strips of metallic gold undercoat. Each of the 6 large sections was divided again into 3 smaller sections. The sawtooth detail on the outside band was made with 33 pointed shapes, cut from a triangular pattern piece that was slightly curved along the bottom edge. The 8-pointed center star was cut in one piece; a second, smaller circle was glued in the middle. Follow these guidelines to create this table, or adapt them for a project of your own design:

1. Cut a circle from birch plywood. If you are applying a separate wood edging around the table, do that now. Fill and sand any flaws in the surface, and gesso or prime the table.

2. Create a paper pattern, either by accurately measuring the angles with a protractor and drawing the lines on a large sheet of kraft paper or by cutting an identical circle shape out of paper and folding it into 6 sections. Draw a circle in the center to accommodate the star motif. Draw the border band around the outside edge.

3. Now that you have established a pattern for the main elements of your design, you can paint or metal-leaf the actual tabletop surface. If you prefer, you can simply cover the entire top. Since in this design all you will see of the undercoat, however, is ¼-inch strips between the main sections of paper, if you are using metal leaf you can specifically treat the areas that will be visible. Leafing or painting in inch-wide strips that follow the lines on your pattern will give you enough undercoat to work over. You may also choose to paint or leaf the edge of the tabletop at this time, although it can be done at the end. Let your work dry thoroughly before continuing.

4. In order to see ¼ inch of the paint or metallic leaf undercoat around the center star, along each of the 6 main sections, and around the inside of the border band, these sections must be reduced slightly in size. To do this, draw a new line ⅛ inch inside the original lines on your pattern.

5. Now divide each of the 6 large sections into 3 smaller, equal sections. These sections will touch with no undercoat showing between them.

6. Using the border band along 2 large sections (one-third of the total tabletop), divide the band into 11 equal triangles. These triangles will have slightly curved bottoms that correspond to the curve of the tabletop. You do not have to complete the other two-thirds since you have now established the size and

shape of your pattern.

7. For the center circle of your pattern, trace the eight-pointed star in the photo above; you can enlarge or reduce a tracing of our star to fit your table.

8. Once you know the exact size of one large section, one small section, the center star, the border band, and one triangular detail, cut these pieces out of the kraft paper to use as a pattern. Using these pattern pieces, cut out all the shapes you will need from the actual papers. We used four different wallpapers in our design. You will need 6 sections of color A; 6 sections of color B; 6 sections of color C; 1 circle of color D and pieces of color D to run around the outside border; and 33 triangular shapes with slightly curved bottoms in color B. Using a compatible color,

run a permanent marker around the cut edges of all the pieces to ensure that no white lines will show in your finished design.

9. Glue the larger circle in the middle of the table. Following the picture above, glue the sections in place, leaving space for the undercoat to show as illustrated.

10. Glue the black paper border around the outside of the table and add the triangular cutouts. Glue the star in the center of the table.

11. Carefully check each piece to make sure that all the edges are securely glued and there are no air bubbles. Loose edges will lift when the tabletop is sealed.

12. Seal the table with multiple coats of sealant (see pages 212–213 for sealant options), and wax with paste wax and a damp cloth, buffing the tabletop to a soft sheen.

Designed by remarkable trompe l'oeil artist Richard Lowell Neas for Brunschwig & Fils, this wallpaper, which perfectly duplicates shelves of colorful and intriguing books, can transform a room into the Harvard Library in a matter of hours. But for a fraction of the investment we created a bibliothèque, chock full of titles, by adding small strips to the doors of this old pine cupboard. The scraps create a witty hatbox with an education marching around the circumference.

ground as described on page 114. Leaf will look like the metal spacers between stone sections on real inlaid tops. Dark or neutral paint will look like grout or mortar. Another advantage to trimming the pieces slightly smaller is that this technique accommodates small irregularities in the measuring and cutting. The ¼-inch blank space allows you to shift pieces slightly and makes lining up the design easier. "Inlaid" tables are like jigsaw puzzles, a characteristic that is part of the challenge and part of the fun.

Other types of furniture

ARTFUL CHAIR

An art print—angled unexpectedly on the back of a Queen Anne Chair—is a whimsical surprise.

Moving from tabletops to pieces with sides and legs requires a lengthier time commitment and some serious planning before a single piece of paper is cut. However, the very same techniques, the same adhesives, and the same range of sealing options apply to large, complex pieces as do to the simpler work of designing and covering flat surfaces. Of course, there are some things, like wood carving or metal ornament, that you cannot cover; but often you can paint out those areas, or gild them, and concentrate on papering the more manageable sections. In any case, most furniture projects require some skill and a great deal of patience.

One problem you will have to consider when you plan to cover a piece completely with paper is concealment of the raw edges. Papers should be applied in an order that places all of the visible raw edges facing away from the front, or main view, of the piece. This means, for example, that you would wrap papers from the sides onto the front and finish the front surface with a cut piece that would be trimmed at the right and left edges. The reverse would leave you

STAR-STUDDED BUREAU

The veneer was chipped and the wood discolored in this American Empire bureau, but the shape was bold and beautiful and perfectly suited to the trio of dark-ground star papers. The design idea here was to color-block the piece like an Amish quilt, but to do so in a way that followed the individual segments and the structure of the piece. If you study the piece carefully, all the places where the colors change make perfect sense, so even though the colors visually break the bureau into parts, they don't weaken its impact. The mirror was a separate find. Gilded and papered, it makes the perfect star-spangled companion!

with the side pieces trimmed at their front edges and those raw edges clearly visible as you look at the piece. To make the cut edge less apparent when you are using a dark ground paper, always run a marker of a similar shade along the cut edges before applying the paper.

You may, of course, simply choose to decorate a piece of natural wood, painted, or laminated furniture with a collection of small cut elements. In this case, you would use the flat surfaces for découpage and not worry about wrapping corners, drawers, or legs. Sometimes it is amusing to allow cutouts to cross a natural barrier in the design of the furniture—the top edge of a drawer, for example—and continue right onto another surface area. You can free the drawer by slicing through the cutout with a very sharp razor after the glue has dried. This is an interesting way to off-center a design and add an element of spontaneity.

It's not always necessary to do serious découpage to embellish furniture. You can use self-adhesive papers to great effect on simple tables, desks, wastebaskets or other such pieces. Self-adhesives are difficult to position, so complicated furniture shapes are really out of the question. But these quick-to-install, inexpensive papers, offered in some really stunning textures and patterns, can make an effective design statement on a slick contemporary piece. And for the really laid-back découpeure, stickers and seals can be pressed onto nearly anything. Combining them in original ways, adding floral garlands around puppy dogs or butterflies, pressing them densely on black lacquered pieces to create neo-Victorian whatnots and curios, is a practically instantly gratifying solution for turning old furniture into your own, personalized, one-of-a-kind!

PAPERED WASTEPAPER BASKET

Interior designers Michael Zabriski and Scott Salvator added the finishing touch to their home office with a paper-covered wastepaper basket, lined in a complementary paper and trimmed with grosgrain ribbons. To cover both faces of the four graduated side panels, eight individual pieces were cut from a cardboard pattern. Any awkwardness at the seam lines on the outside was attractively disguised by the addition of the ribbon, a touch that also serves to outline the interesting shape of the basket.

WHIMSICAL WASTEPAPER BASKET

Lest we get too preoccupied with elaborate, intricately planned, and exactingly executed cut paper work, we show this casual little wastepaper basket. Made by interior designer/découpeure Libby Cameron, this piece with its disparate elements in hither-thither placement illustrates a more relaxed approach to découpage.

NAPOLEON WASTEPAPER BASKET

A dealer of antiques and collectibles had among his treasures a beautiful wooden wastepaper basket from India. It provided us with a perfect base for this sophisticated neoclassical design. You'll recognize the print; it's that favored hand-colored Emperor Napoleon engraving we've used before. This time we enlarged it slightly in the copying to better fit the scale of the basket. The tassels were clipped from a European design magazine.

Découpaged Lampshades and Bases

One of the things we learned while researching this book

was that nearly everyone has a lampshade story. Most center around

a horror that inhabited the front room in a summer rental or the parlor

of a grand aunt. None were too favorable or, for that matter, too tolerant

on the subject of découpaged lamps and shades. Fortunately,

however, there are glorious paper shades to be had, as well as some

beautiful and memorable découpaged exceptions to the peeling

These shades were papered for us at a custom lamp shop in an all-over squiggle print of beige on cream. The printed paper provided a soft and lightly textured background for the skillfully drawn flowers and butterflies we color-copied from some fine old prints and a group of French place cards. Notice the shell finial, made by fixing the coquille to a small finial with quick-setting glue.

FRUITFUL SHADE

These applied fruits once decorated a set of note cards. We cut out the prettiest ones and arranged them around a purchased marble paper shade, using tiny bits of clay to secure them to the shade while we worked on the final design. Once all the pieces were lightly attached with the clay, they could be glued on, one by one, without totally disrupting the overall design and losing track of the spacing.

pink dogwood coolie shade that accessorized Aunt Bessie's back bedroom. We have an abiding respect for the woman whose découpage work first taught us that even though the line between grotesque and gloriously chic can be fine, the lowly découpaged lampshade can reach Olympian design heights. That woman, of course, is Mrs. Henry (Sister) Parish II, the doyenne of interior decoration and herself a skillful découpeure. We can no longer remember which magazine photograph or otherwise immortalized Sister Parish room it was that caused the thought "Now, that's a *lampshade!*" to cross our minds, but wherever or whatever it was, it must have been wonderful because it changed our ideas about découpaged lampshades forever.

The lamp bases and shades in this chapter cover a wide and varied range of styles and designs, and we hope one or two of them will dispel any lingering doubts about their potential decorative charm. There are the requisite animals, fruits, butterflies, and Chinese ladies with fans, but there are also the not-so-usual and the downright rare. The fun of all of this is that lamp base and shade projects are small, challenging you to go right ahead and get creative!

Special paper and découpaged lampshades

When planning a special paper or paper-detailed lampshade, as important as selecting the actual design and decoration of the shade—the colors, papers, cut elements, borders, etc.—are the choices of size and shape and the decision whether the shade will be translucent or opaque, a decision that will influence the aesthetics of the shade as well as the quality of the light.

The first consideration when pairing shades with bases is proportion. The rule of thumb is that the shade at no time be taller than 85–90 percent of the visible height of the base (excluding the socket, bulb, and/or harp). A shade that is too tall looks like an oversized hat. The shape of the shade is a highly personal and very visual decision. A shade is an accessory and must relate—by its shape, color, and/or decoration—to the base. These guidelines are true, of course, whether or not you intend to decorate the shade or the base. The very best way to pick a shade is to bring the base to a good shade shop and try a few different sizes and shapes from stock before deciding.

There is also the issue of opacity. Although translucent shades give more ambient room light, when the light is turned on, découpaged decoration on the shade will tend to disappear because light will flood through the undecorated areas and blind the eye to the design. If there are areas in your design where you have applied one piece of paper over another, even if it's just a slight overlap, a translucent shade may allow the paper underneath to "grin" through the outer layer, complicating or compromising the look of your design or pointing out your mistake. "Skips" where pieces don't join perfectly may also be visible, requiring touch-ups with acrylic paint after the shade is completed and held over the light. Both skips and grin-through are hard to spot during the actual production of the shade; holding the shade up over a light while the glue is still wet, while you can shift the pieces slightly, can minimize these problems. It is also important to mention that translucent shades can cause the color and pattern of applied papers to change significantly when the light is turned on. If you have planned

GLOBAL SHADE

This fiberglass shade was treated with wood stain to look like weathered parchment. Calendar reproductions of antique maps were cut apart, "thinned," and edited to create a design that fit the shade. To prevent little empty areas where sections joined from showing up when the bulb is turned on, we filled in the "skips" with acrylic paint in dark sepia and umber tones.

JUNGLE ANIMAL SHADE

This simple black oval shade was decorated with animals and baroque scrolls carefully cut from two gift-wrap papers. The complicated design was worked out meticulously on the table before a single piece was applied to the actual shade; each little section, or "cartouche," was assembled individually and arranged around the bottom of the shade, spaced in a way that related to the oval shape. Finally, the border was designed, built from individual animal heads and from leaves cut from the scroll-printed paper. We paid special attention to the selection of animal heads, centering a front-facing one on the long sides of the oval, flanked by a left- and a right-facing one, a small touch that makes a big difference in the quality and charm of the finished piece.

NEOCLASSICAL CANDLE FOLLOWER

A metal candle follower was covered with black-and-white marble paper and then detailed with several small black neoclassical urns cut from a wallpaper border. To add sparkle, silver stars of the elementary school variety were lined up along the edges.

STRIPED CHANDELIER SHADES

These chic striped shades were created by applying strips of white drawing paper to purchased black chandelier shades. In order to accommodate the slight slope of these shades and ensure perfect spacing between the "stripes," we cut each white paper strip a bit narrower at the top than at the bottom. The ends of the paper strips were wrapped onto the inside of the shades, where a little extra glue holds them firmly in place.

a shade in the same paper as the walls, for example, and want an exact match, day and night, translucent shades cannot be used successfully. In addition to protecting the clarity of your paper designs, opaque shades allow you to apply a finishing coat of polyurethane or varnish without concern that the brush strokes will show when the light is turned on. Therefore, even though translucent shades give more light, if you intend to seal the shade, if you want to avoid showing overlaps, and if you want to keep your design bright and the colors true at night while the lamp is in use, choose an opaque shade.

The simplest papered shades, of course, are those that have no glued decoration at all but are made from extraordinarily beautiful papers. Crushed parchment paper, stained and sealed, adds to the men's club atmosphere so admired in English-style rooms. And few things are as attractive as the use of handmade marble papers, accordion-folded and set over little metal frames on delicate candlestick bases. We do offer you shade patterns and instructions so that you can make your own if you choose to, or if you have no custom lampshade shop near you; but we have found over the years that using a local shade maker is worth the cost since it allows you to conjure up wonderful paper shades without fuss or frustration. Then, if you choose, you can add cut papers and ornament to your heart's content. Like most things in life, finding someone else to do the nitty-gritty allows you to devote more energy to the creative portion of the job.

Although custom-papered shades provide beautiful backgrounds for découpage, commercially available paper shades in appealing colors are less expensive and can work well. There are also some handsome fiberglass shades

RICH PARCHMENT SHADES

These shades were made from real parchment paper that was first chemically treated, then delicately painted to add to the richness and depth of color, and finally oiled to add to the translucency. They beautifully warm and diffuse the light, turning the room into a welcoming, romantic space.

that can be worked over with great success. Using wood stain, for example, on a basic fiberglass shade appears to "age" the shade, turning it into an elegant background for découpage. If you choose to work on fiberglass, however, wear cotton work gloves to minimize the chance of injury.

Of course, if your room requires a

SHADE "SLIPCOVERS"

A contemporary table lamp with a painted opaque shade was given four new looks by the addition of what we call shade "slipcovers." Each was designed from a master pattern that accurately re-created the size of each of the four sides of the shade. "Slipcovers" are meant to be temporary shades that actually sit atop the original shade.

The version above offers a taste of the Southwest. We cut a camel-colored paper with the look of leather into four panels, each the same height but 1/2 inch wider than the master pattern pieces. The overage was glued to stand up on the front of the shade, and these stand-up "seams" were hole-punched and laced with leather lariat ties, knotted at the top and bottom.

In the version above right an abstract free-form design was created by applying torn bits of brightly colored tissue papers to a piece of heavy-weight tracing paper using a nonwoven fusible web as "glue." To re-create this shade: First, using the pattern as a guide, cut four large pieces of tracing paper for the sides, leaving the right-hand side of each piece 1/2 inch wider than the pattern. Then, iron fusible web onto large

lampshade of an unusual color, custom-painted shades are widely available through custom shops. We use them often, with both the exteriors and the interiors painted, the latter usually in soft rose pink or apricot to flatter skin tones. Painted shades must be opaque because with a translucent shade, the brush strokes will show. If you wish, you can paint shades yourself, coating the shade evenly using a latex paint and a good bristle brush. After the shade has dried for at least 4 hours, apply a second coat. Continue to coat the shade until the surface is smooth and even. Matte colors are somewhat easier than semigloss or gloss, but with practice, any finish will work.

If you choose to make a shade from a pattern, you will have the advantage of being able to decorate a flat piece of paper rather than a curved surface. When we are working with a sloped rather than a straight-sided shade, we sometimes make what we call paper "slipcovers," a trick that allows us not only to work on the flat paper shapes but also to avoid gluing or otherwise attaching the paper to the shade or wire frame. The "slipcovers" are fitted to sit right over the existing shade. Slipcovers are fun to do, and although they are less slick and somewhat temporary, they make a gratifying quick change.

If you are decorating a constructed shade, you may find it difficult to position individual cut pieces on the sloping sides while you are finalizing the design. There are handy nonoily clay or puttylike materials (Plasti-Tak, for example) that will temporarily hold little pieces in place, allowing you to make changes and perfect your design.

With a paper, paper-covered, or painted paper shade as a base, you can then detail as you wish with old, repro-

duction, or copied prints, gift cards, doilies, handmade papers, pressed leaves, or little collectibles such as old stamps. Borders, of course, are wonderfully effective on lampshades. They are difficult to use, however, on any but straight-sided or pleated paper shades since shaped shades will not accommodate a straight-printed strip of paper. If

pieces of colored tissue paper. Peel off the backing paper from the fusible web–bonded tissue and tear out the abstract shapes. Keeping the iron set on cool to avoid wrinkling the paper, iron the tissue shapes onto the tracing paper sides. Crease the ½-inch flaps on each piece and glue them with rubber cement to the left side of the adjoining piece, creating the "slipcover."

Near left: These dusky tinted rice papers are barely attached to one another, secured at several crucial points with a tiny amount of rubber cement. We simply tore them in an interesting way, overlapped them, and temporarily fastened them to one another while we adjusted the shapes with a low-tack masking tape. When we liked the way they related to the shade and to one another, we strongly creased the pieces into folds and secured them to one another in several places with rubber cement.

Below: Kraft paper was cut to fit the shade, top and bottom, with approximately an inch overage left at each side, and the adjoining extended sides were then glued together with the seams on the outside. We tore the glued seam overages to create the rough, decorative edges.

LEAF PAPER SHADE

Designed to blend quietly into the room, this papered translucent shade was made from a leftover piece of the extraordinary leaf paper used on the walls. Because it is not opaque, the look of the shade changes dramatically when the lamp is lit. Then the leaf stems, which are barely visible during the day, make a beautiful pattern on the shade.

CHARMING LAMP BASE, OPPOSITE

Light-years away from the staid, precise, and traditional, this découpaged lamp base, made from a clear glass vase, has a fresh, young look. Created by interior designer and découpeure Libby Cameron, the informal placement of cut elements on this piece gives it an unstudied charm.

the shape is slight and the border pattern allows it, you can clip into one edge of the border, making little ¼–½-inch cuts into the pattern. Then you can ease the edge of the pattern, expanding or overlapping the clipped pieces slightly to accommodate the difference in the diameter of the shade as it widens from top to bottom.

Once you've made all the design decisions—selected a ground paper or paint color, ordered or purchased the shade in translucent or opaque, assembled the decorative pieces to be applied, and planned out the design on a piece of scrap paper—the actual work goes quickly. With a ready-made shade and a good supply of odds and ends, a shade that is dreamed up in the morning can be completed before dinner, when you can turn on a whole new look in your room by flicking a switch!

Découpaged lamp bases

The découpaged glass lamp bases we show in this book run the gamut from complicated, exceptional antiques to new, less complex, more easily executed ones. As diverse as the designs may be, however, découpaged lamp bases all start the same way—with a clear glass hurricane cylinder, chimney, or vase. Both hurricanes and chimneys have large openings in the top and the bottom, allowing you to slip your hands inside easily to work. Vases, of course, allow you to work only through the top opening and will require that a hole be drilled by a lamp shop through the bottom to accommodate the cord. Always have the hole drilled before you do the découpage work—just in case! The process of découpaging hurricanes, chimneys, and vases is intricate and demanding, involving many painstaking steps. Since everything that falls between the cutouts and the glass is visible from the outside, there are serious constraints, for example, on the way glue is applied. Découpaged lamp bases require delicate handling and great patience, but you will be creating your own family heirloom.

BLOOMING ROSES

This gorgeous rose-strewn base may look like a fine antique, but it is a contemporary piece, made by the English firm Vaughan. Making a découpaged base is difficult, requiring that you work from the inside with special attention to neatness and precision, but one is a wonderful addition to your room.

GRAPE SHADE

This frivolous little shade neatly fits the flavor of the room. A new paper base shade, cut from cardboard, was covered with kraft paper and embellished with grapes cut from greeting cards and thin paper "cheese leaves" found at gourmet shops. The bottom edge was cut irregularly, following the outline of the leaves and grapes. Using the wire top and bulb clip from an old damaged lampshade as a frame, the top edge was lashed to the old wire frame with a suede shoelace.

MAKING A PATTERN FOR A SHAPED LAMPSHADE

You can use this technique to cover an existing shade, or to create a new shade using salvaged top and bottom wire rims from an old frame. This shade was made from kraft paper that was reinforced with a poster-board base and lashed to the top of an old wire rim with leather laces. Follow the same step-by-step guide to create a shade of your own:

1. The easiest way to make a pattern for a shade is to wrap a piece of kraft paper around an existing shade of the desired shape and size. Tape this cone of paper so that it will not unroll. Note that the edges of the paper will not match up.

2. Cut away the excess paper at the top of the shade, leaving an inch or so for minor adjustments. Rough-cut the bottom the same way.

3. To establish a seam line on the pattern, fold back the pointed end and draw a line on the surface beneath from top to bottom along the fold. Cut off the triangle created by the fold and trim the paper underneath ½ inch beyond the pencil line to allow for overlap.

4. Trim the top edge of the paper flush with the top of the actual shade. If you are making a shade with an irregularly shaped bottom edge, trim the excess from the bottom of the paper, leaving enough to accommodate the deepest part of your design. To do this, hold the paper-wrapped shade up to the light and pencil in the bottom edge of the shade to use for reference when positioning your cutouts. If you plan a straight bottom edge, trim the paper flush to the bottom edge of the shade.

5. Remove the tape and unroll your pattern. The pattern piece for any slope-sided shade will be fan-shaped. Trace the shape onto decorative paper and cut out. If necessary for stiffness, cut cardboard or poster board also and glue them together.

6. Working on a flat surface, position your cutouts along the bottom of the shade and glue them in place. Then trim the bottom of the shade following the cutouts.

7. Roll the shade into shape and glue the back seam securely, fastening it with paper clips until it is totally dry.

8. If you have chosen to lash your shade to a frame, punch holes every ¾ inch around the top edge of the shade, ½ inch down from the top, using a grommet hole punch for small holes or a standard hole punch for large ones. Holding the old wire rim inside the top of the shade, lash the shade to the rim with leather thongs, ribbon, or cord. Tie or knot the ends. Alternatively, use a hot-glue gun to attach a shade to a wire frame, finishing the top and/or bottom with a thin strip of matching or contrasting paper, grosgrain ribbon, or gimp.

You can make a pleated paper lampshade from a wide variety of papers including wallpapers, marble papers, handmade and art papers—even gift-wrap. The prerequisite is that the paper be stiff enough to hold a crisp, sharp crease. If the weight of the paper allows, you can add a border to the top and/or bottom of your shade before pleating. To get a crisp, sharp fold, use a plastic ruler or smoother, or your fingernail, to make the crease. These shades are designed to rest unattached on a purchased wire frame or over an existing shade. Finish the top of your shade with traditional cords or ribbons of varying widths. The following are guidelines to use in creating your pleated shade:

1. To determine the dimensions of the paper you will need, measure the height of the shade or frame you will use as a base along the sloped side. Add ¾ inch to that measurement. This will give you the required width. Then measure the circumference of the shade base and multiply it by 2.25. This figure is the length your paper should be before pleating. If the paper you have chosen is not long enough, overlap and glue two pieces together to get the necessary length. Cut your paper to the required measurements.

2. If you have seamed the paper, begin pleating with a fold along the overlapped seam line and accordion-fold to both ends. We used ¾-inch folds on this candlestick lampshade. If you are making a large shade, the width of your folds can be increased slightly. If you are using a striped paper, the width of the stripes may determine the size of the folds.

3. To join the ends of the shade, overlap a fold and glue it in place. Cut away any leftover paper at the join.

4. To make the holes along the top edge for a fine cord or ribbon, use a tool designed to punch holes for grommets. In a small shade, the holes should be ¾ inch down from the top edge. For larger shades with heavier cords, use a standard one-hole paper punch and place the holes proportionately lower.

5. To determine the amount of cord or ribbon you will need, measure the circumference of the top of the frame and add 20 inches for a bow. Lace the top of the pleats, tie a bow, and place the finished shade over a wire frame or base shade.

DECOUPAGING A GLASS LAMP BASE

Découpaging a glass lamp base is a demanding process, requiring meticulous preparation and attention to detail, good skills, and patience. Like most craft projects, however, if you are organized and proceed slowly, you can manage the technical requirements and create something truly special. Adapted from the classic process taught by the brilliant Hiram Manning, here are the basic steps for découpaging a clear glass hurricane or chimney:

1. Select, seal with aerosol fixative, and carefully cut out all the elements for your design, arranging them printed side up so that you can easily find and reach them as you work. Collect a bottle of all-purpose craft glue, a small container of water, and a damp sponge and put them within easy reach.

2. Finalize your design on the outside of the glass, using little bits of nonoily clay to temporarily secure elements to the glass. Begin with the largest, most central motif and work out from there. When you are satisfied with the design in the round, remove all but the first motif, placing the pieces on the table in groups that reflect your design plan. Remove the clay.

3. Starting with the central motif, place the cutting on the outside of the glass, holding it in place with your finger to determine where you will need glue.

4. Dip your fingers in the glue and spread it on the inside of the glass where the cutting is to go. Now dip your fingers into water and work the water into the glue until the glue/water mixture is the consistency of melted butter or oil.

Keep your fingers clean with the damp sponge.

5. Press your central motif against the glued area inside the lamp base, right side toward the glass. Move it around until it is in the exact position you choose. When it is in place, use your damp, wrung-out sponge to "tamp" the cutting flat against the glass.

6. With the cutting facing you, roll and press the piece with your fingers from the center of the design out to the edges to eliminate all air bubbles.

7. When all the air bubbles are gone, run the damp edge of your fingernail around the edges, pressing from the paper toward the glass. Make sure the edges are firm and tight to the glass; otherwise, paint will run under the edges when you paint the background.

8. Continue to apply the cut-out elements around the whole glass base, following your design plan. If glue begins to dry on the surface of the glass as you work, moisten the area with a wet finger and rub into the glue until it is oily again. Add a bit more glue and continue your design.

9. Because the interior surface of the glass is shaped and the cuttings are flat, the edges may adhere but the center of the motif may pull away. If this happens, soak one side loose and poke in a little glue and a bit of water. Wring out your sponge in hot water and dampen the motif so that the paper can expand enough to adhere to the curved surface.

10. After your entire design is

glued in place, wipe off the excess glue on the exposed glass area and let the piece dry completely overnight.

11. Using a damp sponge wrung out in hot water, wipe from the edge of each paper cutting toward the clear glass to remove every last bit of glue so that the glass sparkles. Let it dry.

12. With a small pointed brush, seal every edge of your design with glass sealer (available at craft shops), brushing it partly onto the paper and partly onto the glass to seal the paper edge and the glass surface. Let the sealed surface dry thoroughly.

13. Select a japan-base oil paint to fill in the background between the découpage cuttings. Stir your paint to eliminate lumps or scum. Using a ¼-inch flat soft-bristle brush, dip into the paint and wipe off any excess on the lip of the jar; to prevent the paint from running under the cut pieces, you must work with a rather dry brush.

14. Hold the base with the design facing you and begin by applying the paint to the edges of the cuttings, pulling the paint out onto the glass. After all the edges are painted, fill in the open areas of plain glass, still working on the inside of the base. To prevent your arm from being covered with paint as you work, start in the middle of the hurricane and work in circles around the cylinder until you reach one end. Turn the hurricane over and repeat this process from the middle to the other end. Do not be concerned about brush strokes; they will disappear with the next coat of paint. Allow the paint to dry thoroughly before applying the sec-

ond or, if necessary, third coat.

15. To make the lamp base opaque (so that the wiring won't show through), line the base with thin aluminum foil, torn in rounded pieces the size of a half dollar. Use full-strength all-purpose glue applied to the dull side of the foil, and glue on overlapping pieces to cover the entire inside of the base. For this process, it is

again easier to start in the center and work out toward the two ends. Trim the excess foil at the edges flush with the rim, top and bottom.

16. Using a soft ½-inch brush, apply a thin layer of protective sealer over the aluminum foil. Then apply two coats of varnish, allowing it to dry for one day between coats.

17. Clean the outside of your lamp base before wiring and adding the base and cap.

Ornamented Boxes, Trays, and Tabletop Accessories

Since the earliest days of découpage, boxes and trays

have been favored surfaces for beautiful cut paper work. Trays are

really tabletops in miniature, flat and inviting for intricate cut paper

work. Lightly sealed and waxed, they provide distinctive accents when

propped against walls, hung like pictures, or placed on

This old oak box is lined in tin and was probably used to hold tea or tobacco. After a light sanding, we applied laser copies of some "billets-doux" from a collection of old, yellowed love letters, allowing some of the rich grain of the wood to remain uncovered. The stamp box came from a craft store. We removed the nondescript metal clasp at the front of the box and covered everything but the hinges with old canceled stamps. Both pieces were sealed with several coats of McClosky's Heirloom Varnish, chosen because it tends to yellow slightly, giving them a consistent golden glow.

tabletops where they can be admired. When heavily protected with varnish or polyurethane, they are useful and practical additions to your home, whether complementing your tea service or presenting the hors d'oeuvres. Like trays, box projects are generally small and manageable, although working on boxes can involve some tricky wrapping of corners and cutting around hinges and other hardware. Paper-wrapped or -ornamented boxes make wonderful accessories. They adorn tables and bookshelves, organize your paperwork, brighten a closet or armoire, or give simple storage a facelift. And both boxes and trays, enhanced with cut papers and memorabilia scraps, make wonderful personalized gifts.

Boxes and storage containers

TRADITIONAL DÉCOUPAGE

Made by one of Sister Parish's talented daughters, D.B. Gilbert, and currently in the collection of Albert Hadley of Parish Hadley Associates, this traditional découpaged metal box is an extraordinary accessory.

You can work on many different kinds of boxes, from wood and metal to cardboard. Our personal favorites are the old wood ones we find tucked away in secondhand and consignment shops, some of which have so much character they dictate the appropriate decoration. When selecting old boxes for découpage, pieces with undistinguished heritage or slight damages are the best candidates. They offer the patina of age without the responsibility of working with an heirloom. If you are planning to create an heirloom of your own, you will want to completely refinish the box, stripping away the old surface and starting fresh. If, on the other hand, you are making a decorative accessory, you can sand, gesso or fill, and paint an old box with flaws and chips, turning the irregular surface into a pleasing base color without stripping it. If you are covering a wood box completely with a

ANTIQUE TARTAN PAPER BOX

Vintage tartan-patterned wallpaper from Secondhand Rose gives this old oak tobacco box with its battered tin lining the look of an antique tartanware box like those shown from John Rosselli's private collection. Like many of the authentic boxes, ours features a black-and-white engraving, which we laser-copied from an old French print and applied on the lid. The little tassels that appear to hang from the lock were cut from a wallpaper border. The tartan picture mat makes a stylish frame for a family photo, turning a plastic box frame into a handsome accessory.

JAPANESE PAPER OVAL BOX

Using a group of handmade Japanese papers, we covered this graceful oval box we'd made from a craft store kit. Little shapes torn from metallic papers were applied as added decoration. The box was lined with gold-leaf paper, grommets were punched in the sides, and a metallic gold cord provided a glittering finishing touch.

MEMORABILIA/SOUVENIR BOXES

Memorabilia, or souvenir, boxes can function like scrap books but without the trouble of gluing in all those ticket stubs and programs and postcards. Covered boxes can also provide out-of-season storage for small accessories. Just save good-quality dress, shirt, or other gift boxes —the kind with real lids—and cover them with a favorite paper, punch in grommets, add ribbons, and you've got a personal filing system with great decorating potential.

PICNIC GIFT BOX

This quick project makes a lovely hostess gift. The art was cut from an old cookbook and glued onto the raw wood top. Then, using a marking pen and drawing pencil, some shading and a shake of "pepper" were drawn in by hand to give the cutouts additional dimension and an impromptu, artistic air. Finally, it was carefully sprayed with several coats of quick-drying satin varnish.

LIBRARY MAP BOX

Once upon a time, this shallow wooden box held Valentine chocolates. The box was so wonderful, it was kept and used over the years for storing road maps. Now, with a page from a calendar of antique maps smartly glued to its lid and the body of the box relacquered with golden-toned varnish, the old candy box has become a cocktail table accessory.

BORDERED BOXES

Judy Straeten, the archivist at Brunschwig & Fils, created these storage boxes from roll ends of papers and bits of borders from the extensive Brunschwig collection of wallcoverings and border papers. As an added fillip, she lined them with copies of old astrological charts.

LEAF BOX

This wonderful raw wood, three-tier stacking box from IKEA was so graceful and well proportioned that we decided to leave all but the top undecorated. The paper we chose incorporates real pressed leaves on a kraft-paper ground. To accent the shape of the box we applied a small strip of a border along the outside edge. Because the veins and crumbled points of the leaves are slightly raised from the surface and in places the stems stick out, it is impossible to completely seal the paper. In order to protect it, however, we sprayed several coats of a clear découpage sealant over the whole surface.

NAPOLEON BOX

An inexpensive, lightweight craft store box in a pleasing oval shape provided a base for this stylish neoclassical box. Created as one of three projects featuring the same nineteenth-century hand-colored engraving of Napoleon, laser-copied to the perfect size for each, this little box makes a delightful tabletop accessory. The gold "beads" around the print were made with a gold marking pen and then smudged to give the piece a little age and authenticity. The box was lined with a copy of an old handwritten manuscript.

paper or papers, the surface needs only to be sanded to even out the most serious dents and flaws, and then washed off carefully before any glue is applied. We love designs that allow some of the old wood to show through, adding natural warmth and a softly varied tone. Even inexpensive new wood boxes, some as humble as the raw pine ones sold at craft stores, can be given instant status with applied papers. Since the wood is not beautiful, you would probably choose to cover them completely or to paint them before applying cutouts.

While we're on the subject of the humble, consider the lowly cardboard box. Dress, shirt, and gift boxes of all sizes and shapes can be covered completely in papers and recycled as fabulous closet storage or memorabilia boxes for stashing old photos, invitations, playbills, etc. Use only really sturdy ones, however; the collapsible kind are hard to cover and generally too flimsy to be worth the effort. Office supply and stationery stores offer heavy-duty cardboard boxes designed for file and paper storage. These boxes are made to last, with good, strong lids and interesting details like metal label holders. Customized with your choice of paper or cutouts, they make sensational open-shelf storage. This is a way to get organized with style.

Then there is the whole wide world of bandboxes and hatboxes, another favorite Lang/Robertson room accessory. You can create a bevy of room-coordinated hatboxes, using both plain and printed boxes as a base. This is a perfect place to use leftover yardage from borders, roll ends of prints, shelf edging, paper napkins with dye-cut "lace," and all sorts of accumulated paper paraphernalia, turning cardboard boxes from kits, catalogs, or variety stores into glorious storage containers. Once you have

established a pattern and cut out the paper details, you can cover a dozen hatboxes in a couple of evenings, transforming your closet or armoire from a cluttered eyesore into a showcase.

Trays to treasure

TRAY AND MATS

Fish cut from a natural history book decorate a small plastic tray to coordinate with a set of purchased placemats with homosote faces and cork backs that got a sharply graphic mitered wallpaper treatment.

KITCHEN TRAY

A brand-new sleek metal tray from IKEA provided a simple and utilitarian base for this project. Using black-and-white copies of colored drawings from a favorite cookbook, we customized this tray to fit right into a modern black-and-white kitchen. One bright accent, the red radish, put the kick in the design. Each of the overlapping pieces of veggie art required cutting away what lay beneath, since some copies become transparent when sealed. The pieces were glued with white glue thinned with a little water and sealed with a high-gloss spray sealant designed specifically for découpage.

Trays, whether wood, plastic, or metal, old or brand-new, make perfect surfaces for small-project découpage work. Of course, extremely valuable trays should never be worked over; antique trays with damages, chips, or other such slightly marred surfaces, however, make very special découpaged pieces. We routinely scour the consignment and secondhand shops in our area, and occasionally we find really fine old trays, sometimes with beautifully hand-painted or -carved details. Brand-new wood or metal trays with interesting shapes can also offer a good background for découpage. With new trays, of course, there is little prep work; only a light sanding to help the receptivity of the surface to glue.

Working on nice old pieces requires careful handling and an equally careful selection and placement of cut elements, all chosen to be compatible in period and style with the tray itself. Using metal trays with hand-painted borders, for example, encourages you to isolate cut and applied elements in the center of the tray, relating to the retained painted edge. You might even consider working into the painted sections by applying small bits of paper that integrate your center design into the existing border, as we did on our Napoleon tray (see page 148). The moment we saw that tray in the shop of a favorite dealer, we knew it was perfect. The soft green ground, the weathered gold, the leaf detail—it longed for the addition of

SERVE AND STORE SET

This wooden tray and set of graduated band boxes feature the same all-over basketweave paper. Individual fruits were cut from a luscious border and applied as decorations. A glass top protects the tray, but it could be sealed with polyurethane as well.

NAPOLEON TRAY

This tray is a perfect example of how new découpaged material can be successfully combined with an old hand-painted design. The tray was purchased in excellent condition from an antiques dealer and needed no work at all. Using one laser copy of the nineteenth-century hand-colored engraving of Napoleon Bonaparte, and dozens of little "pearls" punched out of a border with a hole punch, we integrated the old with the new. The costly nineteenth-century print was laser-copied in three sizes to be used on three individual projects. Using modern technology in this way can add an extra dimension to your creative thinking and design planning, allowing you to multiply whole prints or certain elements from prints, enlarge or reduce sizes, and slightly alter colors.

DÉCOUPAGED PRINT TRAY

Our client had just purchased a small collection of superb nineteenth-century prints depicting nymphs in flowing garments, dancing and cavorting with cherubs. We planned to do a beautiful tray, designed to be used in the room where the prints were displayed, so before framing the prints, we had them carefully laser-copied, making several copies of each. From these multiples we isolated specific elements, such as a swag of fabric from a banner on one of the prints, to create a border. The tray itself was shaped, and by repeating the swag and using figures that related to the tray shape, we designed a piece that captures the feeling of the art and looks as fine and as rare as the prints themselves.

those pearls and that particular print.

Other times we begin with the design elements and then search for the tray. One client had a series of exceptional nineteenth-century grisaille (tones of black, gray, and white) engravings. We searched until we found a lovely old metal tray with a shapely edge and ample oval exterior. The edge reminded us of the swags and folds of the soft classical garments worn by the nymphs in the engravings. We had the tray stripped and lacquered black. Before framing the prints, we made laser-copy multiples. Then we cut out individual elements from the copies and created a new design. The découpaged, varnished, and paste-waxed tray is frequently used for drink and hors d'oeuvre service in the room where the framed engravings are displayed.

HORSE TRAY

This late-nineteenth-century wood tray had an inlaid shell motif in the center and serious moisture damage in several places. In order to minimize the roughness caused by the open grain and the marquetry inlay, we applied several coats of gesso to the top and sanded each coat before applying our laser-copied print and mitered wallpaper border. When we tried using varnish on a scrap of the border, incidentally, the paint ran slightly, causing the checkerboard to blur and take on an old, slightly worn appearance that worked perfectly with the look of the print.

TEA TRAY

This metal tray, vintage 60s, came from a consignment shop. We had it sprayed with a fresh coat of black paint and then highlighted the edges with gold metallic wax, rubbed on with a soft cloth and buffed. We découpaged the top with a small "tea service," created with individual pieces of the printed "Lunéville" porcelains and borders we'd appliquéd on the walls, and sealed them carefully under several coats of latex urethane, chosen because it will not yellow the cutouts.

TOLE CARD TRAY

This tray was quite old and nicely hand-painted in a rich Indian red with gold detailing. By arranging cards from a deck printed with figures in the style of eighteenth-century chinoiserie directly on the surface, small chips and a burn mark were effectively covered. To "age" the cards and make them more compatible with the old tray, we sealed it with several coats of varnish to which we added a tiny dab of both ocher and sienna artist's oil paint. Last, we applied beeswax over the entire tray and buffed it to a handsome sheen.

INSTANT TRAY TABLE

This early-American wood tray was too valuable to its owner to découpage. Instead we assembled a removable design on the top by combining two birthday cards—a charming dog and a Victorian flower basket—placed over a compatible gift-wrap base. When we were satisfied with the arrangement of these elements, we dropped a piece of ⅛-inch glass over it all, and that was that!

Guests are always charmed, and find the fact that it was made with copies of the old prints both surprising and amusing.

Whether old or new, trays made from heavily grained wood may need to be sanded carefully and sealed with a coat or two of gesso before lightweight papers can be glued to them. Otherwise, visible marks from the woodgrain may show through. This is particularly true if you have had the tray stripped, since stripping opens up the grain and causes valleys in the surface that will be very apparent after the piece is sealed. If, however, the prints or cutouts are heavy enough and your surface is relatively smooth, you can glue right over wood just as you would on metal.

Since many wood trays have straight rather than sloping sides, you might also choose to have a piece of glass cut to drop down into the tray to protect the finish from moisture. In fact, if you like the idea of quick-fix decorating and want to embellish a tray in a more temporary way, using no glue or sealer, you can simply arrange cutouts on the top of the tray and then cover them with a piece of glass. In this way you can change your tray design just as you might change the linens on a table.

Tabletop accessories

FAUX MARBLE OBELISQUE

This plaster obelisque was purchased slightly damaged from a home furnishings shop. It was painted matte black, a perfect ground for sleight-of-hand decorating with self-adhesive vinyl papers in four shades of faux marble. On each of the four sides, the colors of the shapes switch, so that although the design stays the same, each facet is subtly different.

Who would ever think that découpaged plates could bring practical beauty to the table or that découpage could provide a clever way to personalize placemats and service plates? Or that an obelisque covered with lowly self-stick marble papers by the yard could become so chic that it accessorizes a bedroom with the ultimate Central Park view. Here are some more of the little wonders that gave découpage its cachet and can add magic to your home.

DÉCOUPAGING CLEAR GLASS PLATES

Jered Holmes, the very talented and creative artist/découpeur who created the plates, opposite, shared his techniques with us. Jered's style is relaxed; his results are spectacular! To make these plates, use clear glass plates, which are widely available in round and octagonal shapes. Round plates require that you curve and overlap the border elements; octagonal plates offer a series of eight straight sides that intersect, allowing you to work with sections of border, shelf edging, stripes, etc. Be prepared for a little mess—this not a tidy job!

1. Assemble your tools and supplies before you begin to work. You will need all your trimmed cuttings and other elements for découpage, white craft glue, scissors, a wooden wallpaper seam roller, a tube of brown and a jar of black acrylic paint, brushes, polyurethane, marking pens (metallic pens are particularly effective), metallic wax, fine-textured sandpaper, washable adhesive-backed flocked paper, and a woven kitchen towel.

2. Begin with the central foreground motif. You will work from the foreground to the background. Spread undiluted craft glue on the back of the plate over an area large enough to accommodate the cutting. (You may also spread the glue directly on the cutting if you prefer.) Press the motif in place, and using the small roller, press excess glue and air bubbles out from the center to the edges of the cutting. The woven kitchen towel is useful for smoothing the cutting.

3. If you are using a border, cut out the sections you will be gluing so that the elements can overlap to accommodate the circumference of the circle or the angles on the octagonal plate shape. Metallic paper doilies work well for this purpose. Cut apart the outside scallops of a doily and arrange the sections to fit. Glue on the sections one at a time.

4. The background between the central motif and the border can be filled in with additional cuttings or embellished with lines, squiggles, circles, crosshatch markings, etc., drawn in with metallic or other permanent marking pens.

5. After all cuttings are applied and dry, squeeze on a little more glue along the rim of the plate and spread it around with your finger, sealing the border where it joins the plate rim.

6. When the plate is dry, lightly sand the rim and brush on black acrylic paint over the entire back of the plate.

7. When the paint is dry, apply two coats of polyurethane over the back. Let it dry completely.

8. Trace the base of the plate onto the back of a comparably sized piece of self-adhesive flocked paper and cut it to size. Peel the paper off the backing paper and stick it in place. The flocked paper will cover only the base of the plate. The paint protects the border.

9. To finish your plate, rub metallic wax onto the edge of the rim with your finger or a soft cloth. Repeat this process a second time for a richer finish. You may choose to sign and date the back border of each plate with a metallic marker.

MAKING A LINED ROUND BOX

Constructing a box from scratch gives you the freedom to engineer the size to accommodate a favorite border or printed paper, or to fill a special storage requirement for dishes, hats, etc. The only tricky part is cutting two perfect circles from cardboard. If you are intimidated by this, check with a local framer. Most will do it for a modest charge, using their foolproof tools. Then follow these directions:

1. You will need a top and bottom circle, a lid edge, and a box side, all cut from cardboard. All of these dimensions are established by the size of the base of the box. Cut (or have a shop cut for you) two circles, one for the body of the box and a second, $1/8-1/4$ inch larger, for the lid. Because the lid must fit over the box and accommodate the thickness of the paper you will use to cover it, the lid circle must be slightly larger than the base circle. To determine the length of the piece for the sides of the box, first measure the circumference of the circle and add 1 inch. Then decide how deep your box will be and cut your side piece to this width. The piece for the edge of the lid should be the circumference of the lid plus 1 inch in length and approximately $1-1\frac{1}{2}$ inches wide. You may, of course, choose to make the edge of the lid wider to fit a special border or paper.

2. To make a lined box, begin by tracing the top and bottom circles onto the back of the paper you are using for the exterior of the box. Then cut out the paper circles $1/2$ inch larger than the drawn lines. Next, trace the cardboard circles onto the back of the liner paper and cut them out $1/8$ inch smaller than the drawn lines.

3. Roll or brush adhesive on the back of the exterior paper circles. Center and glue them on the corresponding cardboard circles. Clip around the edges at least every $1/2$ inch to allow the paper to wrap onto the back of the cardboard pieces. If you need to, run a line of adhesive along the outside edge of the back of the cardboard circles and press the paper "tabs" firmly into place. Be sure that the paper is securely glued, with no air bubbles or wrinkles. When the glue has set, center and glue the liner paper circles onto the back of the cardboard pieces, covering all the tabs.

4. Trace the cardboard shapes for the lid edge and the sides of the box onto the back of the exterior paper. Cut the paper $1/4$ inch larger than your drawn lines. Then trace the same shapes onto the liner paper. Cut the liner paper $1/8$ inch smaller than the drawn lines.

5. Roll or brush adhesive onto the back of the exterior paper pieces for the lid edge and box side. Lay them flat on a surface and place the corresponding cardboard pieces down on them, leaving $1/4$ inch allowance all the way around. Smooth out any air bubbles or wrinkles. With the cardboard side up, wrap the $1/4$-inch allowance over the cardboard and miter the corners by pinching together the paper from the adjoining sides and snipping it off with scissors. When the edges are securely glued and flat, let the pieces dry a little. Apply the liner papers, centering them on the cardboard pieces. Sometimes, heavier-weight liner papers will wrinkle when you form the side piece into a ring. If your liner is heavy, glue a piece on a scrap of cardboard and curve the cardboard, checking for wrinkles. To avoid wrinkling, you may have to apply the liner paper to the box side after you have overlapped the back seam. In this case, you must apply any decorative cutouts on the assembled sides, not with the piece laid flat as described below.

6. The four completely covered cardboard pieces can be laid flat and decorated with cut papers, borders, etc. (If you choose, or if you have applied the liner to the side piece after it was overlapped, you can glue the decorative cutouts to the assembled box.)

7. To assemble the box, use a hot-glue gun and a clear glue stick. Place the base circle, the smaller of the two circles, lining side up on a flat surface. Wrap the box side piece around the outside of the circle as tightly as possible, overlapping the ends. Draw a line along the edge of the overlap. Run a line of hot glue down the seam allowance from the pencil line to the edge of the piece, and glue the overlap in place, making a ring. Reposition this ring around the base circle, and while resting it on a flat surface, run a line of hot glue on the inside where the sides meet the base. This will secure the base circle to the sides.

8. Repeat this process for the lid.

9. If you choose to finish the box with grommets and ties, follow the instructions included in "Covering a Round or Oval Box," beginning with step 11 on page 138.

COVERING A ROUND OR OVAL BOX

Covering an existing round or oval box with paper is an easy and satisfying project. In addition to providing attractive storage and making charming accessories, covered boxes are an excellent and economical use for leftover borders, papers, and trimmings. Before covering a box, check that the lid is slightly loose and will accommodate the thickness of the paper you want to use. If the lid fits tightly, don't wrap the paper to the inside; cut it flush with the bottom of the edge. Adding grommets at the sides, threaded with ribbons or cords in matching or contrasting colors, gives a box a professional look. Here are directions for covering an existing round or oval box of any size:

1. To cover the body of the box, measure the height of the box and add 1 inch. Measure and cut a strip of paper as wide as this measurement and long enough to wrap around the box plus ½ inch overlap at the seam.

2. Glue the paper around the box, leaving ⅝ inch overhanging the top edge and ⅜ inch overhanging the bottom edge. Smooth out all wrinkles and air bubbles with a plastic smoother.

3. Clip the paper at the bottom edge every ½ inch or so to allow it to wrap onto the base of the box. Apply a line of glue along the outside edge of the bottom of the box, and using your thumb to crease them and press them firmly into place, glue all of the little paper tabs down securely.

4. Turn the ⅝-inch paper allowance at the top to the inside of the box, wrapping it snugly over the edge. Depending on the paper you are using, you may need to clip it several times around the circumference to make it lie flat against the inside of the box. Do this only if it is necessary to prevent wrinkling. Glue the folded edge securely in place.

5. To cut the circle of paper for the bottom, put the box down on the wrong side of your paper and trace a line around it. Cut out the circle ⅛ inch in from this line, making a circular piece that is slightly smaller than the actual bottom of the box. Glue the circle onto the box and smooth it. As always, sponge off any excess glue.

6. Covering the lid involves the same steps as covering the body of the box. Measure the height of the lid and add ⅞ inch. Measure the circumference and add ½ inch for overlap at the back seam.

7. Glue the edge strip of paper in place, leaving ⅜ inch at the top and ½ inch at the bottom. Clip the overhanging paper at the top every ½ inch or so to allow the paper to lie flat, and glue the tabs securely onto the top of the lid.

8. Turn the ½-inch overhang at the bottom of the lid to the inside, wrapping it snugly over the edge. Again, depending on the paper you are using, you may need to clip it several times around the circumference to enable it to lie flat against the inside of the box. Do this only if necessary to prevent wrinkling.

9. Cut a circle of paper to fit the top of the lid, tracing from the actual lid and subtracting ⅛ inch all around as you did for the bottom

portion of the box. Glue it in place and clean away any glue residue.

10. If you are adding cutouts to the box, apply them now. Clean off any excess glue and allow the box to dry thoroughly.

11. Put the lid on the box in order to establish the placement of the grommets. On one side of the box, mark places for three grommets in a small triangular arrangement with the apex of the triangle falling just below the bottom of the lid. Remove the lid and measure the distance from the top of the box to the apex grommet. On the opposite side of the box, mark this distance down from the top for a single grommet. Install all four grommets. If the box you are covering already has grommets, press the wet paper into the grommet to outline it, let it dry, and then cut carefully around it with a craft knife to expose the entire grommet.

12. Measure across the top between the grommets on opposite sides of the box and add 12 inches to determine the length of cord or ribbon you will need. To add the cord or ribbon, put a knot in one end and pull the other end through the single grommet, leaving the knotted end on the inside; pull it across the top of the box to the apex grommet on the opposite side; thread it through the apex grommet from the outside to the inside; bring the cord inside the box to either one of the remaining two grommets and thread it through to the outside; then thread the cord through the remaining grommet from the outside to the inside; knot the cord. The cord should be slack enough to allow for a "handle." Replace the lid. The cord will keep it securely in place.

Personalized Frames, Pictures, Mats, and Mirrors

Frames, picture mats, and mirrors can be immeasurably enhanced

with papers, borders, and cutouts. Picture or mirror frames with enough

flat area on the molding can be covered or detailed with any

paper you choose, from wallpapers that match or coordinate with the

room to beautiful handmade papers, leafed papers,

SHAVING STAND WITH MIRROR, PREVIOUS PAGE

This antique shaving stand mirror is framed in English oak turned to resemble bamboo. It was purchased from a dealer on the original, but now broken-down, stand. In this reincarnation, however, it sits prettily on a bamboo bureau, decorated with a group of rose-strewn place cards, bits of gift cards, and the corners of dye-cut stationery that looks like lace. Laser-copied Victorian greeting cards were applied to the backs of the brush and mirror and then sealed with several coats of specially formulated acrylic découpage spray sealant.

MATTED BOTANICALS

These frames were all purchased ready-made; the smaller ones from a craft store, the larger from IKEA, where they were offered in standard European sizes. The IKEA frames were a bit too tall for their width, and in order to use standard-sized botanical prints, we had to adjust the dimensions of the mats, creating a disparity between the width of the mat at the top and bottom and the width at the sides; a difference that became even more apparent when we added the decorative border. A narrow strip of fall-away from one of the hatboxes papered for this room, however, filled the gaps, top and bottom, and solved that problem. In order to better integrate the narrow strips and disguise the miters (which were unsuccessful after several tries), we cut a small floral element from an unused section of border and applied one on each corner. The four small botanicals were enhanced by the addition of a row of "pearls," cut from the same border paper, and picot ribbons, glued right to the mats.

marble papers, and so on. Wood frames, which we use most often, are particularly well suited to this use. You can have new frames made at a framer, choosing a molding with some flat areas, or search out old ones. There are always solid old frames—attractive but with undistinguished heritage—stacked around at antiques shops, secondhand shops, and garage sales. The old ones are more interesting and are generally sold at a reasonable cost. Borders, either of the exact size needed or trimmed to fit, are naturals for decorating frames. Since borders are designed to have a narrow pattern, they are generally more interesting than a slice of an all-over printed paper, and mitering them at the corners contributes an additional punch to the design. We also recommend a touch of gilt on narrow edges of the frame, a detail that highlights the applied papers. A thin line of gold, silver, or metal leaf will also set the frame off from the wall in an attractive way. This is a place where metallic gold- or silver-leaf paints or waxes can be used to great effect and with less fuss than real leaf. Running a line of paint or applying metallic wax with a soft cloth or a finger along thin edges will, with a minimum of effort, add a lot of dazzle and glamour to your work.

If you prefer to work on a frame that has already been covered with paper, there are myriad papered frames available through catalogs and at good stationery, photo, framing, or specialty shops, all of which provide excellent background papers for découpage.

You can always apply small cuttings to a frame, either over papered areas or on their own over natural wood or a painted ground. Découpaged frames incorporating flowers, butterflies, and other small elements are traditional; you can, however, produce some very con-

DÉCOUPAGED MAT
This charming printed collage came bound right into the holiday issue of a shelter magazine. By combining it with butterflies and flowers cut from gift-wrap and a narrow strip of marble paper applied to a yellow mat, it makes a lovely accessory.

temporary frames using torn papers or unusual bits that work well in a less traditional room. These highly detailed frames are particularly successful when used with a mirror because, unlike art or photographs, a mirror brings nothing competitive to the design of the overall piece.

If all you are adding is a strip or two of paper, it may not be necessary to seal your work. When you have applied small elements and elaborately embellished the frame, however, you should seal it just as you would a piece of furniture or a small accessory. (See page 212–213.)

Decorative picture mats

TARTAN BOX FRAME
Using the cardboard inset from this Plexiglas box frame as a pattern, we traced its shape onto the back of a scrap piece of the vintage wallpaper we'd used on our "tartanware" box. After cutting it out, we secured it to the cardboard with some double-face tape. Then we trimmed out the center of a watercolor of a proscenium arch, printed on the cover of an old theater playbill. Into the opening went a family photograph, taped into place, and the whole thing was assembled— one, two, three.

Picture mats, those flat, heavy papers or boards that surround pictures, are another excellent background for papers and découpage. Mats, both white and colored, can be cut from Bristol or mat boards and be covered completely with paper, be decorated with narrow bands of papers or borders, or both. You can create your own French mats by gluing on thin strips of marble paper and then outlining them with colored or metallic markers. Narrow borders can be used successfully on mats, of course, as can a variety of cutouts. When you are working with small strips of paper or border on a colored board, the color becomes part of the design. Ribbons can also be applied to mats in combination with paper strips for an easy and effective embellishment.

Mats can be purchased precut in standard sizes from photo, stationery, specialty, and some housewares stores. The advantage of precuts is that they come with the openings cut at an angle, called a "bevel." Bevels add a professional look to the mat and can be further

DRESSED-UP FRAMES

Readily available (and inexpensive) acrylic box-style or stand-up frames are easily customized with mats embellished with mitered borders, medallion cutouts, map prints, or custom cut wallpapers. Marble papers and gift wraps in complementary colors can be glued directly to the frames themselves.

Personalized Frames, Pictures, Mats, and Mirrors **165**

detailed by the addition of gold- or silver-leaf paint or metallic wax along the diagonal edge. You can purchase a special tool with an angled blade for cutting bevels; they are tricky to use and require some practice, however. Framers will usually agree to cut mats in custom sizes for you (even if you are providing your own frame), will tighten up old, wobbly frames, and will put the whole thing together for you at the end. In our opinion, this is money well spent.

Mats not only decorate but add importance to your framed art. Choosing a mat in a sharply contrasting color will confine the art and visually hold it to its actual size, no matter how large the frame. A mat in a similar tone, however, can expand the visual size of the art, giving it impact and a more impressive scale.

Other decorative frames

Slick contemporary frames are both widely available and inexpensive. Glass clip frames, for example, are attractive and a cinch to decorate, either by using one large piece of paper against which you center the art or photo or by detailing them with borders and cutouts. Plexiglas box frames, which consist of cardboard boxes that fit snugly into plastic trays, offer a quick framing and decorating fix. As with clip frames, a large piece of paper cut to the same size as the cardboard insert will make an instant mat or background for the art or photo. You can also add borders or decorative cutouts to the paper background. You cannot, however, use wallpaper or art paper to embellish the edges of the cardboard insert since paper will tear when the insert is pushed back into the tray. You can use

SISTER PARISH...
TWO COLLAGES

A funny little zigzag frame complements a "décollage" by Sister Parish. A delightful addition to this tabletop arrangement, this work brings an unstudied charm to a sophisticated room setting. Another of Mrs. Parish's wonderful pieces highlights a second demilune table in the same room. Both are in the collection of Albert Hadley of Parish Hadley Associates.

COLLAGE COLLECTION

A group of intriguing collages made up of prints and found objects such as lace, shells, coral, coins, and threads by artist Jered Homes decorated a long wall in the home of the designer. Some of Jered's fabulous work-in-progress clutters his table with cutouts from auction catalogs and magazines, scissors, and glue.

strips of self-adhesive paper on the edges, or to cover the entire top of the box and wrap around to cover the edges. Lightly spraying or brushing on paint will also disguise the edges of the box. With both glass clip frames and box frames you can use double-face tape to hold the elements in place until you press the second piece of glass or the plastic tray into place. This eliminates any gluing and saves time and effort. These frames welcome decorative experimentation.

An easy way to add impact to framed art or photography is to "hang" it on walls or screens, using appliquéd paper ribbons, swags, and bows that you glue on in the appropriate location before hanging the art from a picture hook or nail. There are scores of paper bows, rosettes, and other such elements, sold by the set, the pair, or the piece and designed to look like the real thing. You can also cut individual pieces out of borders and papers and adapt them for this use. The trompe l'oeil effect is charming and enhances the importance of the framed art on the wall.

Yet another way paper can decorate a room is in art, either representational or abstract, created from cut or torn paper. Called collage, or as Mrs. Parish refers to her work in this medium, "décollage," such works can range from the purely decorative to those of museum quality. These paper "pictures" can be contemporary in feeling, like those made by the gifted Jered Holmes, or quite traditional. The "theorem" collages from Ursus Prints were made from original hand-colored engravings and are quite serious, both in style and in cost. The extraordinary Sister Parish and her talented daughter Apple Bartlett create "décollage" pictures that, when framed, make ingenuous and charming works of paper art, bringing

liveliness and humor to a room. And for Helen Cooper, an interior designer, the line between art and decoration blurs when, using the nineteenth-century art of photomontage, she applies beautiful photographs directly to the wall and turns a hallway into a permanent gallery. Here, as in traditional print rooms, the application of art has itself become the witty design theme.

Découpaged mirrors

Mirrors offer another decorating possibility. This is the technique we call the "mirror/glass sandwich": pressing papers and cutouts between a thin piece of mirror (called shock or single mirror) and a thin (⅛-inch) piece of glass. Shock mirror is very thin and almost impossible to find. Most glass and mirror dealers do sell double-thick mirror, ⅛ inch thick, which will work in nearly all situations. When purchasing mirror for découpage, the thinner the better. Thin mirrors reflect less of the back of the cutouts, and of course they weigh less. By placing cutouts between a thin piece of glass and a thin piece of mirror, you can create a beautiful project without laborious gluing and sealing. The découpage elements are lightly placed on the mirror with a dab of glue and the glass presses them into place. The only requirements are that the total depth of the "sandwich" be no greater than the depth of the rabbet in the frame, so that the mirror/glass can be set flush into the frame, and that you scrupulously clean them, leaving no fingerprints or dabs of glue on either the mirror or the back of the glass. Once it is mounted in the frame, no one will know how you did it and it's guaranteed to generate positive comment on your level of skill.

CLASSIC DÉCOUPAGED MIRRORS

These lovely decorated mirrors feature meticulously cut butterflies and flowers applied over a rich golden yellow painted ground. Created by our friend Mary Havlicek, they are perfect examples of traditional-style découpage.

STAR MIRROR

This mirror cost all of $15 at a secondhand shop. The raised stars in the corners inspired us to create a suite: the mirror and a bureau to match. We had the edges gilded with Dutch gold-leaf papers and ran a narrow strip of star paper along the frame. The mirror and bureau are a great team, brightening up a blank wall with style and storage.

TROUT MIRROR

This humorous mirror is the pride of the Robertsons' fishing camp. Bought because it was decrepit and worn, the unretouched frame with its tarnished gold and oak combination now holds a "sandwich" of mirror and glass. Between the slices are two trout, cut from reproduction prints, a cut-out fly, and a real piece of old linen line clipped from an antique reel, with a selection of bugs, newts, and frogs marching around the frame.

CREATING A "SANDWICH" MIRROR

"**S**andwich" mirrors are made, as the name implies, by sandwiching cutouts between a piece of mirror and a piece of clear glass, both cut from ⅛-inch or thinner material. After you have assembled your mirror, the "sandwich" will be placed in a frame with a rabbet, or recess, deep enough to hold the thickness of both pieces, mirror and glass. To make a sandwich mirror, follow these easy steps:

1. Before cutting, blacken the backs of all the paper elements you will use to decorate the mirror with a soft black pencil. This prevents the cuttings from reflecting in the mirror, showing the white edges. Obviously, blackening before cutting eliminates the risk of tearing off small parts with the pencil. After the backs are penciled, cut the elements.

2. Lay the cut-to-size mirror and glass on a flat surface. Arrange the cutouts attractively on the mirror. When you have finalized your design, lift the pieces one by one, apply a small amount of glue on the center of the backs, and place them face up on the mirror. If you need to mark the position of any overlapping cutouts, use a water-soluble glass marker to make tiny marks.

3. When everything is lightly glued into place, completely clean away all finger and glue marks, first with hot water and a sponge and then with an alcohol-moistened cotton ball. Let the glue dry.

4. Clean the glass as described above. Place it over the mirror, and holding the two pieces of glass

together with a little tape, take the "sandwich" to the framer. If you are mounting the mirror yourself, be sure to fill in the remaining depth of the rabbet in the frame with cardboard, both to hold the mirror/glass snugly in the frame and to cushion the mirror. A side-shooting staple gun is the best way to secure the mirror/glass in the frame. Most frame-it-yourself shops have both the materials for a frame and the correct tools with which to assemble them.

5. When the mirror/glass is installed, cover the back of the frame with heavy-duty kraft paper to protect your work from dust.

A TINTING TECHNIQUE TO "AGE" PAPERS

If the elements you have chosen for your découpage are reproduction prints or are for any reason too crisp and white for the look you want, you can use a tinted varnish finish coat to "age" the papers after they have been glued. Here are some tips:

▪ We have successfully combined cutouts from various sources by using tinted sealants. Keep in mind, however, that if you start out with several degrees of tonal difference in your cuttings and add a tinted varnish over the finished work, you will end up with deeper tints but the same degree of tonal difference among the elements. This technique works best, therefore, for elements with the same or very similar ground colors that you simply want to tone down to an aged, mellow glow.

▪ You can tint cutouts before applying them to a surface by sealing them beforehand with a tinted sealant. This is a way to make elements with varying ground tones work together: Tint the whiter, paler ones and leave the older ones as they are. Rather than spraying them with clear fixative, brush on a sealant you have tinted with tube colors in brown or sienna as described below. Never use shellac, either tinted or amber, for this purpose since it is not compatible with many varnish finish coats and will cause the varnish to lift from your work. Special découpage sealants are available for this purpose.

▪ Always remember to test sealants before applying them. Some colored prints, magazine clippings, and wallpapers will run if treated with some sealants. Try some on an inconspicuous corner or a scrap first.

▪ Amber-colored varnish straight from the can will, after several coats, build up a mellow patina. The depth of the amber color depends on the varnish and the number of coats you apply.

▪ To enhance the amber tone of varnish or polyurethane, add a small amount of oil or acrylic color to the sealant. Be sure to select a compatible medium: oil for oil-base sealants, acrylic for latex or water-base sealants. Van Dyke brown, burnt sienna, and ocher are all good choices for tints. You can, of course, experiment to get a tone you like. Thin the tube color with water or turpentine and add it to the sealant, enough for one coat at a time. The darker the sealant, the richer the color. This is a good formula for one coat:

¼ inch of tube color (acrylic or oil)

1 teaspoonful of thinner (water or turpentine)

½ cup of sealant (latex or oil-base)

TOOLS, TERMS, AND TECHNIQUES

PART 3

What is a half-drop? When does using wheat paste lead to disaster? What in the world does a brayer do? This section will help you to understand the more practical requirements of creating rooms and accessories with the look of those photographed on the previous pages. Even though each project is unique, requiring some inventiveness and often some experimentation, there are practical guidelines and technical caveats that can make the work more pleasant and help you avoid costly and frustrating glitches and errors. Most of the projects in this book are within the reach of the weekend paperhanger and the first-time découpeur. This section will provide you with information on what tools you will need, what terms you must understand, and what you need to know technically to accomplish these projects. Here are some of the tools, the words, the materials, the common-sense procedures . . . the tried-and-true tricks of the trade.

Tools of the Trade

Having the right tool for the right job can save hours of effort

and help you achieve more professional-looking results. Here are our checklists

of the indispensable tools for large wallpapering jobs

and for small découpage projects.

Tools for wallpapering

WORKTABLE: The simplest and least cumbersome worktable for cutting and gluing rolled wallpaper is one you make from a pair of sawhorses with three 6–7-foot 1-× 12-inch boards laid side by side on top. This gives you a large work space that is wide enough for all commercial papers but is easily disassembled and stored. A single sheet of plywood placed on a base is extremely heavy and cumbersome to move and to put away. Another good worktable is a hollow-core door, which, although it doesn't knock down to store as the board table can, is lightweight.

LEVEL: A large 4-foot level can immediately help you to determine the straightness of both your seams and the horizontal pattern. You can also use a plumb bob to check the seams, but it must be suspended from a nail, which will leave a hole.

STRAIGHTEDGE: Commercially available 8-foot metal straightedges can be cut down to the length of your worktable. Use them to trim the sides of untrimmed papers.

T-SQUARE: A metal T-square can slide along the straight edge of your table, ensuring a straight cut at the top and/or bottom of a strip of paper.

TRIANGLE: A metal right-angle triangle is very useful for ensuring straight vertical cuts and for creating miters.

SCISSORS: The best for cutting rolled papers are large, sharp, and heavy. Commercial paperhanger's shears make long, clean cuts. You will need smaller sizes for smaller jobs, everything from standard paper shears to 5–6-inch scissors, to manicuring scissors for delicate trimming around printed patterns for custom-cutting borders. The most critical thing is that your shears and scissors are sharp and make cuts that are neat and clean.

RAZOR BLADES: The secret to perfect blade cuts is to have a huge supply of fresh razor blades. Buy them by the hundred at paint and paper stores. This is particularly important when you are cutting into wet paper.

MAT AND CRAFT KNIVES: Mat knives may be used instead of razor blades, which are difficult for some people to hold and handle. Craft knives are perfect for small cutting, such as cut-out bottoms on borders.

BROADKNIFE: Not a knife per se, but a tool meant to provide an edge against which a razor cut can be made. It can also be used to scrape old wallcovering off the walls.

SMOOTHERS: There is a wide selection of smoothers available at paint and paper stores. The ones we like best are plastic and about 6 inches wide. Metal smoothers can work for heavy vinyl papers, but they will

outside corner rollers, designed to reach into and roll over these difficult areas without catching and tearing the paper. Rollers are made from bone, vinyl, or wood.

RULERS AND TAPES FOR MEASURING: A measuring tape is, of course, indispensable to determine cut lengths. A folding wooden carpenter's rule can help to measure wall heights since it is somewhat free-standing against the wall and can be handled by one person.

ROLLERS AND PAINT TRAYS: This rudimentary painting equipment is necessary for applying prep coats to the walls before the paper is installed.

SCORER: A wheel on a plastic or wood handle, this tool is rolled over old paper to score it, allowing water from a sponge to seep behind and loosen the paper from the wall. Scorers are sometimes called paper tigers.

SPONGES: Clean sponges are used for wiping glue from the surface of papers as you work. Large soft sponges work best.

mark the surface of and easily tear through nonvinyl ones.

SMOOTHING BRUSHES: Meant to gently and easily smooth papers and vinyls, these brushes come in various styles and types. They are a must on delicate papers where plastic and metal smoothers can cause marks or tears.

ROLLERS: Straight rollers and barrel-shaped rollers secure the wallpaper against the walls, particularly at seams. There are also inside and

Tools for découpage

WORKTABLE: Any clean, perfectly flat table will do. You might use a wood cutting board or one of the self-healing boards specifically designed for use with small blades. They are available at art supply stores.

GLASS GLUING SURFACE: A small piece of $\frac{1}{8}$–$\frac{1}{4}$-inch glass, approximately 12 × 18 inches, with its edges safely taped with heavy masking tape, is an excellent surface on which to apply glue to tiny cutouts.

STRAIGHTEDGE: A metal ruler is good for small work.

T-SQUARE: Small-scale metal T-squares are available at art supply shops.

TRIANGLE: A small metal triangle can be useful for cutting angles or mitering.

SCISSORS: The most important tool for small work. You will have to discover as you work which lengths and types are easiest for you to handle. Five–6-inch scissors, mustache trimmers, and manicuring scissors for delicate, curved cutting are nearly indispensable. Buy the very best scissors you can afford and keep them well sharpened. Most fabric shops provide sharpening service.

RAZOR BLADES: You may want to use them for straight cutting, although paper shears work just as well on these smaller jobs.

MAT AND CRAFT KNIVES: Mat knives work well on larger cuts, but swiveling craft knives, once you've got the hang of using them, work well for very small curved work. They can be used in place of manicuring scissors to make intricate cutting easier.

SMOOTHERS: Six-inch plastic smoothers will work well on most small work, particularly when used over sheets of wax paper to hold the pieces down while working out excess glue without wrinkling or tearing tiny edges. You can also use your fingernail.

WALLPAPER BRUSHES: Sometimes the smallest of these are useful. Be careful, however, that they don't leave too much glue under the papers. Sometimes using your fingers on small, delicate work is the only good way to gently press it into place, particularly with laser cop-

ies, which tear easily.

BRAYER: A brayer is a traditional découpage roller. It is small, made of rubber, and available at art and craft stores. Used with wax paper, the brayer allows you to roll over small pieces and secure them firmly in place without wrinkling or tearing.

RULERS AND MEASURING TAPES: Any small-scale rulers and tapes are useful. Clear plastic rulers allow you to measure without blocking the work underneath.

CHEESECLOTH: Cheesecloth is used damp for cleaning glue off the surface of delicate pieces.

Glossary of Terms

The following is a list of the terms, technical and common, we have

used in this book to describe the process and the materials used in

decorating with papers.

APPLIQUÉ: From the French for an "applied" element, this term describes the process of gluing individual printed elements to a surface or object.

BITE: Roughness created on a surface by the application of primer or sizing to encourage good adhesion between a paper and the surface.

BLIND CORNER: A corner in a room in which mismatches can most easily be hidden, usually behind a door.

BOIS: French for wood. "Faux bois" refers to printed papers that closely resemble woodgrain.

BOLT: The package, or "put-up," in which wallpaper is sold, usually in double or triple rolls.

BOOKING: The technique of folding wallpaper strips back to back after pasting, to allow the adhesive to soak into the paper.

BORDER: A narrow, decorative strip of wallpaper, generally used along the ceiling line and around window and door openings. Very useful for decorating accessories as well.

BUTTED SEAM: A seam in which the edges of wallpaper strips meet exactly, edge to edge, without overlapping.

BUTTERING: The process of working thinned white glue with the fingers until it is the consistency of butter or oil. A term used when working on glass, such as lamp bases.

CHAIR RAIL: A strip of decorative wood molding mounted approximately 29 inches off the floor, meant to keep chair backs from scraping against the wall. Can be created with borders to visually separate one section of the wall from another.

COLLAGE: From the French *collager*, to paste up. Used to describe a painting that incorporates cutouts of paper, newspaper, bits of string, wood, or any other item the artist chooses to incorporate into his or her work. Also, a work made up entirely of paper cutouts and other glued items.

COLOR RUN: A batch of wallpaper rolls printed at the same time, using the same inks or dyes. Since colors will vary from color run, or "dye lot," to color run, each printing is assigned a run number. When ordering additional rolls, therefore, it is important to order by the run number to guarantee a perfect match.

COLORWAY: A trade term used to describe a particular color version of a fabric or wallcovering. Generally, prints are designed with several optional colorways that use different ground or print colors.

COMBING: A technique whereby a tool called a comb is dragged through various layers of paint or glaze to create a stripe or crosshatch pattern. Combs can be metal or hand-cut from heavyweight cardboards. "Strié" wallpapers look combed.

COMPANION PAPERS: Wallpapers designed as a collection and meant to be used in combination with one another. The group may include several prints or patterns of different scale, a complementary stripe, and a border or two.

COMPANION PRINT: Term describing a print designed to work in combination with another or others in the same design scheme.

CORNICE: See entry for "crown molding."

CORRUGATED PAPER: Heavyweight paper or cardboard that is folded or shaped into parallel ridges or furrows during manufacturing to form a wavy surface.

CROWN MOLDING: The horizontal molding running along the top of a wall where it meets the ceiling. Also called the "cornice."

DADO: The lower portion of the walls in a room, separated by some architectural element, such as a chair rail or molding.

DAMAR VARNISH: A petroleum-base sealant used to protect oil paintings. Can be tinted and used to give an aged, slightly yellow tone to paper work.

DÉCOUPAGE: From the French word *découper*, to cut out or cut from. The craft of decorating surfaces with applied paper cutouts.

DÉCOUPEUR/DÉCOUPEURE: A person who creates découpage.

DÉCOUPURE: French term for a "cut-out." The term was originally used in the eighteenth century by Marie Antoinette to describe her lacy hand-cut mementos.

DIRECTIONAL PRINT: A print with an obvious top and bottom that cannot be successfully installed upside down. Directional prints generally do not work on ceilings.

DOUBLE-CUT: Term used to describe the technique of overlapping two strips slightly at the seam and then cutting through both layers at the same time to produce a perfect fit. After cutting, the waste, or fall-away, is removed quickly and the edges are firmly rolled into place.

DROP-MATCH: Describes one of two basic types of wallpaper patterns, "straight-match" and "drop-match." With a straight-match pattern, the design along the top edge of a strip of wallpaper starts and ends at the same vertical point in the pattern. When the pattern of a second strip is aligned with the first strip, the design along the top edge of the second strip is the same as the design along the top edge of the first strip. With a drop-match pattern (which requires a "half-drop" to match), the pattern at one side of the strip is one-half repeat *lower* than the other edge, requiring that the second strip be "dropped" until the pattern repeats are aligned across the two strips. The designs along the top edges are the same, then, on *every other strip*. Repeats designed in this fashion are called "half-drop repeats."

DUTCH-CUT: Term used to describe the technique of double-cutting an overlapped seam. The two pieces are cut at one time; the cut strips, or "fall-away," are then quickly removed and the edges are firmly rolled into place.

DYE LOT: See "Color run."

FALL-AWAY: The leftover portions of printed papers or borders that remain after sections have been cut out or the paper has been seamed.

FAUX: French for false, imitation. Used to refer to painted or printed finishes or materials that are designed to resemble another, natural surface such as marble, granite, wood, moiré, tile, etc.

FOIL: A metallic film used to create a shiny, polished metal ground for some wallpapers.

FRENCH-CUT: Term used to describe the technique of double-cutting an overlapped seam by hand-cutting a wavy line from the top of the seam to the bottom. This technique works well on large floral prints, for example, where a straight line cutting through the pattern would be more visible. After cutting, the cut strips, or "fall-away," are removed quickly and the edges are firmly rolled into place.

FUSIBLE WEB: An adhesive film that is ironed onto one surface in order to cause it to adhere, after the application of steam heat, to another.

GESSO: A mixture of fillers, acrylic polymers, and thickeners used to prime canvas or other surfaces. Available in white and tints.

GLAZE: A thin mixture of oil and mineral spirits that is tinted before it is applied so that it will add a sheer layer of color.

GLOSS MEDIUM: A polymer emulsion that can be used as both glue and sealant/topcoat, but made without flatting agents so that it dries to a gloss finish.

HALF-DROP: A repeat that requires the "dropping" by one-half on every other strip in order to align the pattern to obtain a perfect match. See "Drop-match."

HAND-BLOCK: The process of using hand-carved wood blocks to apply pigment to papers.

HAND-SCREEN: The process of applying pigments to paper by the use of individualized screens, or "mats."

HANDMADES: Refers to all handmade papers; i.e., not made by machine.

KRAFT PAPER: (Also called "craft" paper.) Brown commercial papers used for wrapping or in the production of brown paper bags.

LAPPED SEAM: A seam in which the edges of the wallpaper strips overlap slightly.

LATTICE: A diamond-shaped, or *treillage* (French), pattern that evokes the look of trelliswork, giving a room the look of a gazebo or garden.

LAUAN: A reddish-brown plywood that comes in various thicknesses, including ¼ inch; it is lightweight and inexpensive. It may be used when weight is important for such projects as screens, but it must be securely nailed to a wood frame to prevent warping.

MARBLE PAPER: Paper made by hand or machine that is designed to resemble marble. Traditionally made by floating oil-base pigments on water, mixing them into a pleasing design, and then dragging paper through the bath. Also called book or end paper.

MATTE MEDIUM: A polymer emulsion specially formulated to be used as both a glue and a sealer/topcoat for acrylic paintings. Dries to a matte, or nonshiny, finish.

MATTE VARNISH: A pale, translucent liquid varnish that dries without shine.

MECHANIC: Term used in the trade to refer to craftspersons such as paperhangers or painters.

MOD PODGE: A trade name for a water-base sealant, glue, and finish coat useful for nearly all surfaces. Mod Podge can be used to appliqué with both fabric and paper cutouts. The work must be sealed with a clear acrylic sealant to eliminate surface tackiness. Available in a gloss-luster or matte finish.

MONTAGE: Literally, French for "mounting." Collage incorporates montage.

PANEL PRINT: A paper designed as a scenic, or mural, and intended to re-create in several panels a pattern or picture. Panel prints are generally printed in 9-foot lengths.

PATTERN MATCH: The alignment of a design on wallpaper strips at the seams to ensure a pattern that matches horizontally all around the room.

PATTERN REPEAT: The number of vertical inches between identical points in a pattern design.

PLASTI-TAK: A puttylike material that is nonoily and nonstaining and can be used to hold cut pieces on an object or surface temporarily while designing and before permanently attaching them.

PREPASTED PAPER: A wallpaper that comes from the manufacturer with adhesive already applied to the back.

PRETRIMMED PAPER: Wallcovering whose selvage edges have been trimmed at the factory.

PRIMER: Refers to the base coat applied to the wall before the installation of wallpaper. Primer seals the wall and acts as a base for sizing. It also facilitates removal of the paper.

PUT-UP: Referring to the lengths in which a particular paper is available from the manufacturer; i.e., single, double, or triple rolls. Some European papers are prepackaged by the manufacturer in longer, 11-yard, put-ups.

RAG CONTENT: The percentage of cotton rag fiber used in the production of a particular paper. Generally, a higher rag content makes a better, stronger paper.

RAILROADING: The technique of installing a wallpaper horizontally rather than vertically as designed. It is appropriate for applying nondirectional wallpapers above and below windows and doors. Intentionally placing the pattern on the horizontal can be an effective way to create a border in a room, either by using the paper in its full width or by cutting into the paper and installing a narrower strip.

REGISTER MARKS: Small shapes of color printed on the selvage of a wallcovering that indicate how many screens, and therefore how many individual colors, were used to print the pattern. Generally, the more screens, the more costly the paper.

ROLLAGE: Trade term referring to the measuring of wallpaper by rolls rather than feet or yards.

SCREENS: The term used to describe the individual mats used to print each of the colors in a screen-printed fabric or paper. Each color in the print is applied separately, one over the other, and each color requires a new screen. The code for the number and color of each individual screen, called register marks, is printed on the selvage. Usually, prints involving large numbers of screens are more expensive than those requiring few screens.

SEALANT: A clear or slightly tinted liquid that, when dry, effectively seals the surface of an object against moisture and dust and protects it from damage. Sealants include varnish, polyurethane, latex urethane, and shellac. They are applied at the completion of the work and cannot be reworked without extensive sanding. We refer to all finish coat materials in this book as sealants.

SEALER: A liquid that is painted or sprayed on a raw wood or paper surface to prepare it for paint or découpage. In some cases, the same product is used for a finish coat; we use the term "sealer" to distinguish the process rather than the material. Sealers will, for example, stiffen paper, making fine cutting easier, and prevent the image from running when glue or the final finishing coat, or sealant, is applied.

SELVAGE: The unpatterned or blank strip along the edges of wallpaper. Register marks indicating the number of individual colors in a print (see above) and marks indicating the match are printed on the selvage edge. Selvages must be trimmed away before the paper is hung. A pretrimmed paper comes with the selvages already removed at the manufacturer.

SIDEWALL: An overall patterned paper, designed as part of a collection that incorporates specialty papers including dado, border, corners, friezes, etc. Also used to refer to an individual small-patterned paper that can be successfully combined with other patterns and elements.

SIZING: Refers to sealers and undercoatings used with wallpaper. Sizing a wall adds to the bite, or tackiness, which in turn helps to ensure a good bond between the paper and the wall.

SMOOTHER: A metal or plastic straight-edged tool designed to ease gently along the surface of a freshly pasted paper in order to push out any extra adhesive, remove bubbles, and secure the paper firmly.

STRAIGHT-MATCH: See "Drop-match."

STRIÉ PAPERS: A French word referring to very delicate, finely "combed" papers that use several different tones or colors to add depth and richness to the color on the wall. Strié papers are designed to resemble elaborately prepped and painted walls to which several colors of glaze are applied, one over the other, and then "dragged" with a tool called a comb to create a pattern.

TACK: Refers to the stickiness caused by sizing, which helps to bond the paper to the wall. Tack should remain even after the sizing solution has completely dried.

TEMPERA PAPERS: Papers printed with watercolor paints. These papers generally require pretreatment to protect them from staining, the use of special adhesives, and special handling during installation.

THINNING: A découpage technique literally used to thin the paper on which decorative elements are printed, by soaking them and then carefully rolling off layers of paper with the fingers.

TISSUE PAPER: Very lightweight translucent papers traditionally used in gift-wrap. Available in many colors.

TRACING PAPER: A translucent paper designed for copying or tracing.

TREILLAGE: French word for trellis, or lattice. Used to refer to lattice papers, which give the look of a gazebo to a room.

TROMPE L'OEIL: French for "fool the eye." Art so realistically rendered that it appears real.

VELLUM: Paper made to resemble a fine parchment, prepared from calfskin, lambskin, or kidskin.

VINYL: A plastic wallpaper, usually backed with paper or cloth. Vinyl wallcoverings are distinct from *vinyl-coated* wallcoverings, which are simply paper treated with a plastic topcoat.

WATERMARK: A mark produced by the pressure of a mold or stamp during manufacturing, visible when the paper is held up to the light. Watermarks identify the maker of the paper and are generally found on handmades.

Techniques for Wallpapering and Découpage

This chapter provides the information you will need

to successfully avoid situations like this one. When you understand

the best ways to estimate rollage the first

time, to select adhesives that stick, to prep walls adequately, to apply papers without flaws, you can eliminate the frustration of a messy defeat. Likewise, after you've learned the guidelines for choosing the elements for découpage, perfectly preparing the surface, selecting appropriate adhesives and using them properly, applying the cutouts without damaging them, and permanently sealing and waxing your work, you'll be ready to dream up some wonderful découpage projects without fear of failure.

Our technical wallpapering information has been accumulated over eighteen years of working with a wide assortment of talented craftsmen. For many of the rooms and projects in this book, we worked with an exceptional one, Charles Puzzo. The secret to his success is that although he knows and can implement traditional procedures, he is willing to throw tradition to the winds and develop new techniques when necessary. He also will keep trying until he finds one that works. Unique among the many painter/paperhangers we've employed, Charlie doesn't think we're crazy when we ask for something he's never been asked to do before. This, as far as we're concerned, is a fabulous recommendation. The knowledge we've gained from our years of working with Charlie and our own experiences with cut and paste have enabled us to provide information that is very personal and, as we know firsthand, will work— whether you do the work yourself or hire a professional.

Our expert on découpage is our longtime friend Mary Havlicek.

Mary has been découpaging for more than fifteen years, and enthusiastically helped us adapt traditional découpage techniques to the quicker, less demanding style we used to create many of the projects included in this book.

Even though there is a great deal of technical information in this chapter, please remember that this is a book about the creative process of decorating with paper. Should you need additional nuts-and-bolts information, you might refer to one of the many excellent self-help books, manuals, and videos available at paint and papering, hardware, craft, or book stores, or your local library. To learn more about the nuances of découpage, we suggest that you check in craft or book stores or your library for books written exclusively on that subject. Some are quite old; they are around because the information is valid and excellent. Some, found only in libraries, are out of print. These books, thumbed over by hundreds of fascinated découpeurs or découpeurs-in-training, dogeared and well loved, were our favorites. Just check under "découpage." The definitive book is *Manning on Découpage* (Dover Publications, Inc.), written by the charming and immensely knowledgeable Hiram Manning. Mr. Manning describes in great detail the classic techniques of découpage.

Wallpapering techniques

"With wallpapering, it's sixty percent prep, forty percent pretty."
Charlie Puzzo, mechanic

Estimating wallpaper rollage for a room

Before ordering paper or borders for a room, you will need to understand the process of measuring and calculating rollage for walls and ceilings and figuring yardage for borders. Here are some important factors that affect your calculations:

AMERICAN ROLLS/EUROPEAN ROLLS: American-made wallpapers generally come in rolls approximately 5 yards long, depending on the width. Each roll will cover roughly 30 square feet of wall surface. Some papers coming into this country from England and Europe are packed in what are called "European put-ups," which are longer than American rolls; they come in 11-yard lengths and cover approximately 55 square feet. In our residential design work, we had one embarrassing situation in which, because we ordered European papers based on the American 5-yard roll, when we looked into the shipping carton after the last wall was installed we discovered enough unopened rolls to do the entire job again. Always check the length of the rolls before figuring out your order.

REPEATS: Some papers have large pattern repeats that can greatly influence the amount of paper required to finish the room. A repeat is the number of vertical inches between identical points in the pattern design. Papers come with the length of the repeat printed on the package. Because repeats must align at each seam, the match could require you to trim off some excess paper in order to continue the pattern along the top, or ceiling line. This excess may total almost as much as the entire repeat. Therefore, when estimating the amount of paper you will need, you should add the number of inches that make up the repeat to the lengths every time you need to make a cut in the paper. Therefore, if the walls are 96 inches high and the pattern repeat is 24 inches, you would figure the panel lengths at 120 inches each. Every time you plan to cut the paper for the installation, including sections over doors and windows, add the repeat. It is possible that you won't need that much leeway to make the matches, but you won't know until you start to work.

DOUBLE- AND TRIPLE-ROLL PUT-UPS: Ordering paper in double- and triple-roll put-ups can save on paper and, therefore, on the job cost. If your ceilings are 8 feet high and the paper you've chosen comes in 5-yard (15-foot) lengths, even with no repeat to deal with you probably will get only one long strip per roll. (A very deep crown molding or an applied border could make the difference). If, on the other hand, you can order the paper in a double-roll put-up of 10 yards (30 feet), you will be able to cut three floor-to-ceiling strips. Obviously, the short pieces can be used over doorways and over and under windows, but long strips do count, especially in a room with few openings.

RUNS AND DYE LOTS: Papers are printed in runs, or dye lots; that is, a certain number of rolls are manufactured at the same time from the same batch of mixed colors. All the papers from the same run will match in color; colors they mix for the next run might be slightly different. These dye lots or runs are usually identified by a number or letter printed on the invoice and on the back of the actual wallpaper. Manufacturers have an allowance for off-color, which enables them to ship papers that have a small variance from their original samples. What this means to you is the following:

Let's say you estimate that you need 12 single rolls of paper for a particular room. A roll arrives damaged or is damaged after delivery . . . or the pattern requires a different placement in the room than you had imagined . . . or the repeat causes more waste than you had calculated. If your estimate was to the inch, you may now be short a roll or two. If the run from which you purchased the paper has been sold out, your additional order will be shipped from the next production run. When the paper arrives, the color is slightly off. In fact, if it is from a new print run, the chances that it will match perfectly are slim to none. There are two ways to deal with this problem. If

you check and discover that you have ordered short *before* hanging the paper and the manufacturer can't supply you with paper from the same run, you can decide where you might be able to hide the new strips (in an entranceway to the room, in the closet, behind a curtain). You can also try changing dye-lots at a corner, since a slight color variation will be less noticeable where the two planes meet at right angles, and paper the entire wall from the new run. Or, you can avoid the problem entirely by ordering extra rollage in the beginning and accepting the fact that you'll probably be moving those two or three extra rolls around from closet to closet for the next five years. We order extra; it's the safest way.

FIGURING ROLLAGE FOR WALLS: To estimate the amount of paper for an entire room, first calculate the number of gross square feet (length of the walls multiplied by their height plus the repeat, if pertinent). Next, figure the approximate square footage of the door and window openings, fireplace openings, built-ins, etc., and subtract that number from the square footage of the room. (Another good rule of thumb is one-half a roll less for each opening.) Divide this figure by 30 (or 55 if you are using European rolls), and you will have a good estimate for ordering. Add 10–15 percent extra, just to be safe.

FIGURING ROLLAGE FOR CEILINGS: When measuring for ceilings, simply figure the square footage and divide by 30 (or 55 for European rolls). The same information regarding match and repeats, of course, applies here. What you don't have to worry about is doors and windows.

MEASURING FOR BORDERS: To measure for borders, total the running yardage, allowing for the proper placement of the pattern and for the repeat. Borders may be sold by the roll in 5-yard or 11-yard put-ups, or by the yard. As with papers, it is always a good idea to add 10–15 percent to be safe.

Choosing adhesives for wallpapers and borders

Once you have selected the paper or papers you will be using, it is necessary to determine the proper adhesive for the job. It is important to note here that wallpaper manufacturers routinely include installation recommendations with each roll, often in the form of a loose instruction sheet. The following are the standard types of adhesives available and the jobs for which they are best suited:

WHEAT PASTE: Wheat paste comes in powder form and requires mixing with water. An organic material, wheat paste is best for untreated porous papers, which tend to stain quickly and easily. Since it is natural and has no preservatives, once mixed, wheat paste will spoil if kept too long. It also might mildew in situations where it cannot "breathe," such as under vinyl or foil papers. Wheat paste will dry shiny and must be cleaned off the surface of the paper quickly and thoroughly.

CELLULOSE PASTE: A high-quality adhesive that is clear drying, odorless, nonmildewing, and will not discolor fragile materials. Cellulose paste is recommended for grasscloths, burlap, silk, and other paper-backed fabrics; all delicate, easily stained fabrics and papers; and those painted with watercolor or tempera paints.

VINYL PASTE: Vinyl paste comes pre-mixed, is synthetic, and is recommended for vinyl papers or fabrics. It provides superior adhesion and, therefore, works well with heavier papers and with paper-backed fabrics. Professional-strength vinyl adhesive is very effective for applying light papers such as gift-wraps to matte surfaces; you may have trouble, however, getting a good bond on shiny surfaces. Vinyl paste will not provide a permanent bond between two vinyl papers for lapped seams. When dry, vinyl paste left on the surface turns to flakes and can be easily removed.

PREPASTED PAPER: Although prepasted paper is manufactured with a thin coating of water-activated adhesive on the back, our mechanics always add a little adhesive to the water, making a thin adhesive solution, to ensure a good bond. This is particularly true when they use prepasted papers for ceilings, where the weight of the paper makes a good, taut bond imperative. Recently a new product called a prepaste activator has come into the market. It is designed to give a more even application of adhesive to the paper, and adds more "slip" for easier positioning on the wall. It also allows more time to work with the panel or sheet without its drying up, making the job less messy.

BORDER ADHESIVE: This paste is specially formulated to give superior adhesion to a paper affixed to another paper, a property that is critical when applying appliqués, borders, and vinyl to vinyl. With border adhesive, you should be able to apply a border to any type of wallpaper. This adhesive, however, dries quickly, and therefore any adjustments on the wall have to be made quickly before the glue sets up. Never allow border adhesive to stay on the face of your work since it is impossible to remove after it has dried.

Preparing a wall for paper

Preparing surfaces for wallpaper is an exacting process. If you take shortcuts, you may be unhappy with the final result or have big problems later on. Use the following guidelines in preparing a room for paper:

REMOVING EXISTING PAPER: Removing old paper is one of the most frustrating jobs we know. Professionals work with special steamers, sprayers, and chemical preparations, and can generally take down old papers quickly. If you decide to do this task yourself, check at your local paint or hardware store for the names of products designed to speed this process. It's important to not gouge out chips and dents with scrapers and other such tools as you work, since these flaws will only need to be repaired before the stripped walls are primed. A handy tool called a scorer, or as one brand is aptly named, a Paper Tiger, aids in loosening layers of paper by punching holes in the surface to allow steam, water, or chemical paper removers to penetrate.

WASHING THE WALLS: After all the old

you select a paint color that matches the ground of your chosen paper, you can minimize the visibility of hairline seam openings, or "seam splits," which sometimes appear as the paper dries and can spoil the job. After priming, apply a coat of a "sizing," a sealing and undercoating used for wallpaper. Some readily available sizing products that provide superior "tack," or stickiness, and will therefore hold almost anything to a wall are Wonder Base and Shieldz Primer from Zinzer and R-35 from Roman Adhesives. Priming and sizing not only will ease the job of hanging the paper but will also facilitate its removal years down the road. Check at your paint/paper or hardware store to determine which product or products are best for your job.

PAINTING THE TRIM: If you are planning to paint the woodwork, wait until after you have primed or prepcoated the walls for papering. Then paint the trim color slightly up onto the wall so that you won't be able to see the undercolor of the walls along the baseboard or window or door frames after your paper is installed.

paper has been removed, carefully wash the walls with clean water or with the same chemical solution you used to remove the paper.

SANDING AND FILLING: Next, fill all holes, including those from picture hooks and nails, and cracks in the walls and around windows, doors, crown moldings, and baseboards with plaster, caulk, or spackle, repeating the process until the repair is perfectly flush with the wall after sanding. Use 220-grit sandpaper to finish the job. Be sure to carefully dust off the walls.

PRIMING OR SIZING THE WALLS: Scores of products have been designed to prime and/or "size" walls for paper. Using an oil-base paint as a prepapering primer will clean up the repaired walls and leave a fresh surface. If the wall has never been painted before, an oil-base primer is critical. Even spots that have been repaired with plaster or spackle should be touched up with primer. Otherwise, you run a risk of blisters appearing under the paper after it has been installed. If

Applying papers to walls and ceilings

Nearly all wallpapers come with installation instructions included on a separate sheet of paper that comes right in the roll. There are also numerous books and videos on the technique of correctly installing particular types of papers. The primary objective, of course, is to cover the back of precut paper strips with the proper adhesive and to apply the thoroughly glue-covered and suitably saturated paper strips to the wall, smoothing out all bubbles and wrinkles and matching the pattern repeats as you go. Keep in mind that if you are working with prepasted papers, the basic procedures are the same; only the gluing changes, as we discussed above. The following are sensible guidelines you should follow to get paper installed successfully:

INSPECTING THE PAPER: Open and reroll each roll of wallcovering with the pattern side in, carefully inspecting it for color and design flaws as you go. Return any damaged rolls to the vendor immediately. Most manufacturers allow you 30–60 days to return damages for an exchange. If you just change your mind or have overbought, you can return undamaged wallcoverings within that time frame, but you will probably be charged a 25 percent restocking charge; manufacturers' policies can vary. It's wise to check before ordering.

USING LINER PAPER: Liner is an inexpensive plain paper (or blank stock, as it is sometimes called) sold by the roll that is generally used over rough, uneven walls that cannot be perfectly prepared. It is also commonly installed under very thin or fragile papers, such as foils, plastic films, or silks, that might otherwise separate from their backing when wet. Since liner paper is highly absorptive, it helps prevent this separation and keeps the adhesive from seeping back through fragile paper-backed fabrics. Liner paper can be installed horizontally, across the walls, rather than vertically so that the wallcovering seams do not overlap the liner seams. Liner should stop ⅛ inch from baseboards, ceilings, and window and door frames to reduce bulkiness in those areas.

MEASURING AND CUTTING STRIPS: If you are working with a patterned paper, first develop your plan for "placing" the pattern effectively in the room as explained in Chapter 1, "Decorative Wall and Border Treatments," on page 45. Now you must determine the vertical placement of the pattern on the wall. Working with a helper, unroll a generous length of the paper, and without cutting it off the roll, hold it up to the crown molding or ceiling line. Then, avoiding strong elements in the repeat, select an innocuous place on the pattern so that slight variations along the ceiling line (caused by the vagaries of construction or structure settling) will be less noticeable. With a pencil, mark the place on the pattern you have designated to be the top edge. Have your helper mark the bottom edge, where the paper meets the baseboard. If you are working alone, you can determine the bottom edge by measuring the height of the wall and transferring that measurement onto the paper, using your mark as the top edge. Mark the bottom edge. Since the person on the ladder will not have a clear view of the pattern, you may choose to be the one standing by and giving opinions rather than the one on the ladder. Now trim this marked piece, leaving a 2-inch allowance on the top and the bottom for maneuvering the strips. Using this piece as a pattern, roll off and cut several strips. Short lengths left at the end of a roll should be put aside and saved for use over and under windows and doors and for covering switch plates.

ESTABLISHING PLUMB LINES: At the center of the room's main wall, draw or chalk a line from the ceiling to the baseboard, using a level and large straightedge or a plumb bob. This line must be perfectly straight. If you are planning to center a seam on this wall, you will line up the edge of your first strip against this center line. If, on the other hand, you are planning to center a strip, measure out from your plumb line to half the width of the strip and draw a second line. You will line up your first, centered strip along this line. You will need to reestablish a plumb line on each wall.

PASTING AND BOOKING: Lay the first strip face down on your worktable. Using a paint roller, apply the adhesive evenly down and across the entire strip. Using a clamp will keep the paper from rolling back up while you glue. Now, lifting the top end, lightly fold the paper back on itself, glued sides together, until the top edge meets the approximate center of the strip. Line up the selvage edges carefully but do not crease the fold. Then fold the bottom end of the paper back toward the center until the bottom edge meets the top edge. (If you are working with long strips, it's sometimes easier to glue and fold half of the strip at a time.) This process is called "booking." It helps to spread the adhesive evenly and reduces water evaporation while the paper "cures," or rests.

CURING: Once the glue has been applied and the paper booked, set it aside to "cure." Curing softens the paper for easier handling; allow it to cure for about 10 minutes.

TRIMMING THE SELVAGES: If the paper you have chosen has unprinted selvages, they must be removed. While the paper cures, place a long metal straightedge lightly along the edge of the pattern, following the guide marks printed there, and using a new razor blade or snap-point utility knife, carefully cut away both selvage edges. Trimming is done while the paper is still "booked," which is why it is so crucial to align the edges precisely when the paper is folded.

POSITIONING AND SMOOTHING: Unfold the top half of the strip of paper, and place it on the wall with the 2-inch allowance resting lightly on the crown molding or on the ceiling and the edge of the strip butting up against the plumb line. Release the bottom half of the folded paper, and using the palms of your hands, slide the strip into place. Beginning at the top of the strip, smooth the paper out from the center in both directions, using a plastic smoother or wide smoothing brush. Check frequently that the edge aligns perfectly with the plumb line and that you have smoothed out any bubbles.

TRIMMING AT CEILINGS AND BASEBOARDS: After the strip is installed, trim the excess paper from the top and bottom edges, using a broadknife against which you cut with a new, sharp razor blade. To do this safely without the risk of slipping and cutting the paper, always hold the broadknife against the paper and cut over it on the top edge and under it at the baseboard. One trick to learn about this procedure is that you never lift your blade from the wet paper once you start to make a cut; cut, slide the broadknife over, and cut farther.

TRIMMING AROUND DOORS, WINDOWS, ETC.: When a strip of wallpaper partially or completely overlaps a window or door, do not custom-cut the strip to fit around the shape of the opening. Hang a full strip, starting at the ceiling line and allowing it to fall right over the door or window frame. Smooth the strip right down to the frame. Using scissors and cutting from the inside of the door or window opening, make diagonal "relief" cuts in the paper, cutting at 45-degree angles from the center out to the corners of the door or window trim. (If the placement of the strips falls in a way that allows you to use nearly full widths of short roll-end strips above or below these openings, make sure that they are applied exactly vertical to ensure a good pattern fit with the next full strip. In order to accommodate slight mismatches, do not trim the short strips until the last full strip has been hung.) Trim away the excess around the opening with a broadknife and a razor blade. These techniques apply for trimming around any obstacle, in-cluding built-in bookcases, mantels, and cabinets.

CHOOSING A SEAM TECHNIQUE: There are three kinds of seams: butt seams, lap seams, and double-cut seams. Butt seams, as the name implies, are made when two strips just touch along their length. Lap seams occur when the second strip is applied slightly over the first, leaving a double layer of wallcovering. Lap seams will not ever work on vinyl papers since vinyls will not stick to one another. We frequently use the third technique, double-cut seams. Both double-cut and Dutch-cut describe the technique of overlapping two strips about ½ inch at the seam and then cutting down the middle of the lapped paper layers to produce a perfect fit. The cut strips, or "fall-away," are then quickly removed, the top piece first and then the second one from underneath, and the edges are smoothed and firmly rolled into place with a seam roller. "French-cut," on the other hand, describes the technique of double-cutting an overlapped seam by hand-cutting a wavy line from the top of the seam to the bottom. This technique works well on large floral prints, for example, where a straight line cutting through the pattern would be more visible. After cutting, the fall-away is removed quickly and the edges are firmly rolled into place as described above. These techniques are designed to minimize the visibility of the seams in the finished room.

SHADING THE PANELS: When working with textured papers, particularly those that are hand-painted, you might notice a slight shading of the color along the roll. Often you cannot see shading until several strips have actually been applied to the wall. These papers work better if you alternate the application of the individual strips, turning every other cut strip upside down so that on the wall, you will join light to light and dark to dark. Obviously, this works only if there is no direction to the texture.

PAPERING AROUND INSIDE AND OUTSIDE CORNERS: Corners, even though they may appear to be plumb, rarely are. Therefore, don't ever wrap around corners; you'll end up with wrinkled paper and a mismatch on the next wall. To paper a corner, divide the strip into two sections and hang them separately, working from a plumb line or wallpaper edge toward the corner.

On *inside corners*, measure the distance from the edge of the last strip of paper to the corner and add ½ inch. Cut the new strip to that width; glue it and apply it, smoothing the ½-inch extra onto the adjoining wall by clipping into the paper at the top and bottom edges as necessary to make the turn. If, for example, you are working with a strip 30 inches wide and have used 15½ inches into the corner, you will have a piece 14½ inches wide left. (If the remaining strip is narrower than 6 inches, use a new strip of paper on the next wall.) To ensure the vertical alignment, restrike a plumb line ¼ inch farther from the corner than your strip, or in this case, 14¾ inches. Lining up the outside edge of the remaining strip ¼ inch in from the plumb line, install it on the wall and into the corner. Since this process calls for overlapping paper in the corner, if you are using vinyl paper it will be necessary to add border adhesive down the overlapping seam. Trim the excess paper from the top and bottom of the strips, using a broadknife and razor blades.

On an *outside corner*, the process is basically the same. Rather than leaving an extra ½ inch on your first strip, however, you should leave a good 1 inch since papers wrapped around outside corners will try to release from the wall. (Heavy vinyls and foils require more than this; 3–4 inches is a better amount.) After you apply the second section, trim as above. Outside corners rarely make a perfect match since they are generally not perfectly vertical.

APPLYING PAPER TO CEILINGS: To avoid spoiling your wall work, hang the ceilings first, running the strips across the room at its narrower dimension to keep them as short as possible. Strips should be cut 2 inches longer at each end to allow you to adjust the pattern along uneven ceiling lines and to wrap it down slightly onto the walls. If you have no crown molding and are planning to apply paper to the walls, trim the ceiling paper, leaving ½ inch on the walls. If you are leaving the walls unpapered, or have a crown molding, trim the ceiling paper flush to the ceiling edge or to the crown, using a broadknife and razor blades. If you are working with a prepasted paper on a ceiling, either mix additional adhesive into the water or use a prepaste activator. Failing to heed this advice could cause a major disaster. Changes in temperature and humidity can cause self-adhesive papers to let go in some areas, and the weight of the paper, acting with gravity, will strip the paper from the ceiling.

Plan the placement of a pattern and/or the seams on your ceiling in the same way that you would plan paper placement on your walls. (See page 45). Create a plumb line against which you can line up your first strip by measuring in from the outside edges of the room along either wall and chalking a line across the ceiling. This, obviously, requires two people to do.

A good trick for installing paper overhead is to accordion-book the pasted paper, folding it back and forth with the pasted side in. Then allow the paper to cure for 10–15 minutes before beginning to install it. By working with as small a folded piece as possible, you make handling the long strips easier.

Papering ceilings is a difficult task, not because it's technically complex but because you work over your head with long strips of paper. Work on ceilings requires a helper.

APPLYING BORDERS TO WALLS: Before cutting lengths of border for walls, determine the most effective placement of the border by unrolling a long uncut length and, working with a helper, placing it up against the main wall. The main wall is either the one most visible when you enter the room or the one with the main seating group. By shifting the actual border along the wall, determine which are the strongest design elements and place them in the most effective place. This is particularly important when using a border against a patterned wallpaper. Try centering the main motif on the wall, checking to see

what happens at the corners. If that placement is unsuccessful, center the midpoint between two main border motifs and see what happens at the corners. Keep in mind that you can hide a little in the corners by adding or subtracting a bit on the next wall. Look at the way the pattern will fall on each wall by moving the unrolled strip of border around to help you to visualize the effect. Of course, even though you can cheat a tiny bit, you will have to keep the pattern running continuously around the room. Plan one corner, the least noticeable (or "blind" corner), where the two ends of the border will meet with an uncontrollable mismatch.

In nearly all instances we can think of, borders should be applied with border adhesive. Border adhesive is designed to hold paper to paper, paper to vinyl, vinyl to vinyl. Be sure to carefully wash away all residual border adhesive from the face of the border and the wall, however, since once it has dried, it is virtually impossible to remove. If your border does come away from the wall when dry, you can always reglue it or, if it is completely free from the wall, soak it to remove the old glue and try again.

APPLYING BORDERS TO CEILINGS: The process for applying a border to a ceiling is virtually the same as for walls. The only difference is that using a border on a ceiling requires that you carefully miter the paper at the corners. For mitering directions, refer to page 60, "Creating Mitered Borders."

CLEANING AWAY EXCESS ADHESIVE: Carefully washing off papered surfaces with a clean damp sponge to wipe away any excess glue is a critical step. Glue can be invisible until after it's dried, which with some adhesives can be too late. Vinyl adhesive can be flaked off when dry; border adhesive is permanent once dried. You can wash most surfaces with a clean damp sponge while the glue is still wet. If you are having trouble with stubborn glue spots, try a 50 percent solution of water and wallpaper remover on a scrap piece first; if it does not damage the paper, apply it with a sponge to the actual surface. Undiluted alcohol will dull the shine of glue-stained areas, but as always, you must run a test on the paper first.

USING SEALANTS AND WAXING PAPERS ON WALLS AND CEILINGS: Normally you wouldn't choose to seal a papered wall or ceiling. Even though a coat or two of polyurethane or latex urethane may sound like a wonderful idea to add luster to a patterned or textured paper, once it was sealed you would be unable to remove that paper from the walls should you decide to change your decorating scheme. Waxing, on the other hand, does offer some advantages on nonvinyl papers. There are some textures that were designed in Italy and were meant to be finished with an application of a thin coat of warm wax mixed with turpentine and linseed oil and buffed to a soft shine. This mixture is extremely volatile, however. Using any good paste wax and a damp cloth, you can achieve very beautiful results without the risk of combustion. We have successfully waxed many ceilings and some walls in this way, leaving the finished rooms with a soft, subtle glow.

Découpage techniques

"Mr. Manning, these cuttings are exquisite!" enthused Donna, holding up one of a series of chinoiserie cartouches. "And those tiny slits you cut in them to let the silver leaf on the back shine through—that illuminates them!"

"Silver leaf?" said the mischievous Hiram Manning, chuckling. "My dears, don't be silly. Silver leaf is too, too extravagant to use on the back of cuttings. I just use the wrappers from Hershey's chocolate. It's a perfect solution for a chocoholic!"

Choosing elements for the design

Many types and kinds of paper and paper cutouts are suitable for découpage work. More traditional materials include prints and reproductions, posters, catalog and magazine clippings; less traditional ones include stickers, seals, gift-wraps, stamps, doilies, shelf edging, laser copies, greeting and enclosure cards, and so on. Even the master, Hiram Manning, admits to using cuttings from *National Geographic* magazines for some of his finest pieces of découpage. One of the freedoms of découpage is that you can mix the styles of the cut elements to create work that is uniquely your own. If the elements and the colors are happy together, you can juxtapose unrelated cutouts, literally putting anything with anything.

As in the selection of wallpapers, where the room strongly influences the choice of paper and border style and colors, in découpage the object to be covered will influence the elements you choose. The following are ideas and guidelines for the selection and preparation of cuttings for découpage:

SCALE: When selecting elements for découpage, consider the scale of the cutouts in relation to the object to which they will be applied. They should be in proportion to one another and to the whole. Delicate pieces call for delicate cutouts; strong pieces can carry larger, bolder elements. Remember, however, that the scale of the original source is really irrelevant since you will be cutting everything apart; you can enlarge small elements by combining them with others; you can cut out portions or details of large elements, trimming or editing them to more appropriate sizes; and you can laser- or photocopy them, reducing or enlarging them to the desired size.

COLOR: Colored prints, clippings, and other elements must relate to the object to be découpaged and to each other. By painting or papering the object, you can, of course, widen or appreciably alter the acceptable range of color in the cuttings. Coordinating or contrasting background color will strongly influence the look of your design. You can choose to make the background a quiet extension of the color or colors of the prints or select a background color that is highly contrasting and therefore tends to spotlight the cuttings.

CENTRAL MOTIF: In designing a découpage project, it is often safest to start with a central motif, a large, eye-catching cutout, and build your design from there. This is, however, by no means a rule. All-over, asymmetrical, or seemingly random designs are sometimes the most successful of all.

ORIGINAL PRINTS: Original prints are rare and costly, and using them for découpage can immediately turn a fun project into an investment. There may be times when you feel that using originals is critical to your project; we do not use them unless they are seriously damaged and their value has been compromised. Cutting out sections of torn, discolored, or otherwise marred old prints is a way of salvaging them and giving them a new aesthetic life. If you have access to fine prints, either those in your collection or some you have borrowed, you can always laser-copy them for use in découpage (see below).

LASER COPIES: Modern technology offers us an alternative to destroying fine old prints for découpage projects. Duplicating your artwork with a color copier allows you to use multiples of the piece in the sizes of your choice without harming the original. It also enables you to cut individual elements from the print to reassemble in a new configuration.

No matter how good the copier, colors will change in the duplicating process, making it nearly impossible to combine the original with the copy in one project. If you work closely with the technician, however, you can adjust the machine, adding or subtracting magenta, cyan, yellow, or black to achieve the best possible color reproduction. These subtle adjustments can also be used intentionally to alter the color of the original when printed in order to match it more closely to the desired color palette of your project. Equally exacting is the process of enlarging or reducing the originals to fit your project. Measure the element to be copied exactly from the original. Then determine the ideal size you will need. Using the two measurements and a proportional scale (usually available at the copy center or at art supply stores), you can figure the exact percentage of enlargement or reduction needed, thereby eliminating chance and the potential of costly errors.

All copies must be sprayed with clear sealer before they are used in order to set the colors and prevent running or fading from the glue and the water cleanup. Even with this process, copies will often become transparent after the final sealing, particularly if you are using polyurethane or varnish applied with a brush on the finished piece. This transparency may allow bright or patterned papers used underneath to show through. Only the tedious process of cutting away the underneath layers before applying a copy will ensure that nothing "bleeds" through.

Working slowly and thoughtfully is important because laser copies are costly. You can, however, simultaneously copy as many separate elements as you can fit on a sheet of copier paper by planning to combine small elements in ways that best utilize the paper sizes offered by your copy center, normally 8½ × 11 inches and 11 × 17 inches.

Many prints, drawings, patterns, and photographs are protected by copyright laws, which restrict their use and make copying them for resale illegal. If you are using copies for projects you will use in your own home or for gifts, it is unlikely that you will encounter legal problems; if, on the other hand, you use copyrighted prints in the manufacturing of products for resale, there is a serious risk of fines or worse.

THINNING OR PEELING A PRINT OR HEAVY PAPER ELEMENT: Unlike laser copies, some reproductions and original prints are too heavy to use as is for découpage. They are stiff and difficult to apply to shaped or curved objects, and even on flat surfaces require scores of coats of varnish or polyurethane to effectively "bury" their edges beneath the sealant. Thinning, or peeling layers of paper from the back of a print or other heavy paper element, is a traditional way to reduce a paper's thickness. This technique will work only if the paper has a sufficient rag content; experiment on an unobtrusive corner.

There are two methods. In one, you first dampen the back of the paper with white vinegar, being sure not to soak the print. Let it rest for a few minutes, and then with your finger or a slightly damp sponge, carefully rub off the backing in layers until the print reaches the desired thinness. Clean away any remaining vinegar with a damp sponge. Alternatively, you can spray-seal the face of the paper several times, allowing the paper to dry between coats. Then soak it in tepid water for 2 or more hours, depending upon the quality of the paper. Remove the paper from the water and place it face down on a smooth surface where you can carefully rub the back with a turkish towel or a washcloth, gently peeling away a layer. Allow it to dry thoroughly before using.

Keep in mind that if the thickness of the individual elements in your design is similar throughout, sealing the work will be quicker and easier. If you are combining, say, prints with gift-wrap, or laser copies with notecards, you are setting yourself up for a long and arduous job of equalizing their respective heights on the surface of your project with sealant. Thinning and/or laser copying may be viable solutions to these inequities.

Presealing and cutting

Traditional methods of découpage require that you preseal all prints and papers prior to cutting and gluing them. This takes a little extra time but is good advice, particularly when you are using laser copies, which can smudge and tend to become transparent under varnish or polyurethane. Not only does sealing your paper elements help to protect them from damage from glue and finishing coats, it gives them body, stiffening them and making them easier to cut. The following are some helpful guidelines for the preparation and cutting of paper elements:

USING SPRAY OR BRUSH-ON SEALERS OR FIXATIVES: Aerosol fixatives will lightly coat paper elements, protecting them from stains or discolorations caused by glue and/or finishing coats. Those designed specifically to seal, rather than "fix," papers must be used in well-ventilated spaces and with extreme care. Even though spraying is certainly quicker and easier than brushing on sealer, you may prefer the latter method. Art and craft stores, particularly those that specialize in découpage, carry brush-on sealers designed for this use. If you are planning to use shellac applied in several layers as a final finish, you can use it at this stage as well, diluted one to one with denatured alcohol, to seal the individual paper elements. Both the white and the orange varieties of shellac will tend to mellow the paper cutouts. Do not, however, seal the paper elements with shellac if you plan to use varnish or polyurethane to seal your découpage work, since they are chemically incompatible.

TESTING SEALERS BEFORE USE: Always try a sealer on an inconspicuous corner of a colored print, wallpaper, magazine clipping, or book print before brushing or spraying it on. Some colors will run; others may change dramatically. Read labels before use and experiment first.

Cutting out elements for découpage

Since the accurate and beautiful cutting of paper elements is the most important aspect of a découpage project, how you approach this task will greatly influence both the experience of creating a project and the finished result. There are traditional techniques for holding and using scissors, and there are types of scissors that work best in particular situations, but in the final analysis, it is practice and patience that transform this labor-intensive step into an enjoyable and relaxing art form. You may choose to cut a little at a time on a day-by-day basis, freeing all but the most delicate parts of cuttings until you are ready to apply them. In this case, you must store the cutouts in a safe and orderly way. Stacking them in boxes or leaving them around on tabletops is not the answer. Hiram Manning uses notepads and tablets as storage places for delicate cuttings of all sizes, tucking the cuttings, one by one, between the sheets. Since these notebooks and paper tablets are white paper, this is a better solution than using magazines or books, where inks can discolor the cuttings over time. Note the subject of the cuttings stored inside on the cover of the pad. Using this system, you should be able to find a cutting months, if not years, later, in perfect condition and ready to apply.

USING THE CORRECT SCISSORS: Since the accurate and beautiful cutting of the paper elements is the most important factor in a successful découpage project, buy the best scissors you can. Some projects require hours of cutting; excellent scissors can make the process easier and more enjoyable. You will need several pairs. For long cuts such as trimming borders, a pair of good paper shears works best. For more delicate and detailed work, a pair of surgical steel manicuring scissors with thin, fine, curved blades is necessary. You might also choose to own a pair of medium-sized scissors with straight blades for less detailed work that requires some control. Do not use your cutting scissors for lifting or positioning glued cutouts; keep another pair for the messy stuff, if you like. The first rule regarding découpage scissors is that you never use them for anything else, and since they will, like a fine pen, adjust slightly to your unique cutting style, never lend them to someone else.

CUTTING TECHNIQUES: Using straight-edge scissors is a skill most of us master long before adulthood; using scissors with curved blades, on the other hand, requires some know-how and practice. For dé-coupage, hold the scissors with the thumb and middle finger, resting them on the index finger, with the curved blades pointing outward (to your right if you are right-handed; to your left if you're a leftie). Now hold the paper you are cutting in your other hand with your thumb on the top and fingers on the bottom. Turn only the paper; do not move the scissors except to open and close the blades. By cutting up from the bottom in this way, working with the curved blades pointing outward and away from the cut edge, you are always able to see the cut line and to follow it accurately. Feed the paper into the scissors; don't push it. Practice before trying this technique on intricate work. Proper cutting with curved-blade scissors actually creates a slight downward slant on the edges, which aids in the sealing of small, delicate pieces to the surface.

SEQUENTIAL CUTTING: The proper sequence for cutting a print or other paper element is to do all of the interior cutting before trimming away the outside paper. This allows you enough paper to hold on to as you work. To begin an interior cut, push the point of the scissors through the face of the paper, making a slit. Then, working from underneath as described above, continue to cut. Before you start to cut away the outside edges of the element, you may need to leave strips of paper between branches, tendrils, stems, etc., to temporarily connect them to one another and eliminate the risk of their tearing off. These connectors, called "bridges" by some découpeurs, stabilize the cuttings until you are ready to glue them into place.

Preparing a surface for découpage

The preparation of a surface for small work is similar in many ways to the preparation of walls. It also requires meticulous work. The surface must be as clean and smooth as possible. Even small chips and bumps will show through découpage, and flaws that are nearly invisible in unsealed work will show very clearly after you have applied varnish or polyurethane. Follow these guidelines to properly prepare a surface for découpage:

PREPARING A WOOD SURFACE: If you are working on a wood surface that has previously been finished, you may choose to remove all of the old finish with paint or varnish remover before sanding, sealing, and applying your cutouts. Sometimes, however, washing an old wood piece with denatured alcohol and then lightly sanding it to make it more receptive to glue without stripping it of its "patina" is more aesthetically pleasing. When working over antique wood pieces, for example, particularly painted ones, we choose to leave as much of the original finish as possible, allowing it to lend its charm to the project. With new, raw wood, first seal the surface with a generous coat of sealer, allow it to dry thoroughly, and then lightly sand. If you are not planning to paint or paper the object prior to découpaging, you may need to apply more than one coat of sealer to new or stripped wood, sanding after each one. Avoid using shellac at this stage since it is incompatible with most finish coats, particularly varnish.

PAINTING OR PAPERING A WOOD SURFACE: If you are planning to paint or paper after refinishing and sealing, first fill any holes or imperfections with water putty; sand, clean with a tack cloth, and apply a coat of paint primer. Alternatively, you might choose to use artist's gesso. Putty and primer will do the job if the piece is in reasonable condition. Thick, quick-drying artist's gesso fills in any serious nicks or gouges in a distressed finish but requires a good deal of sanding to smooth it out after it dries. After priming or gesso-ing the piece, lightly sand and apply several coats of paint in the desired background color, allowing each coat to dry thoroughly and sanding after each. If you are covering the object completely with paper, prime it, and after it has thoroughly dried, apply a sizing product to ensure a good bond. Sizings that remain tacky when dry work only on objects that will be completely papered. All products used in preparation and painting must be compatible; check your selections carefully by reading the labels and, if possible, experimenting on scrap.

PREPARING A METAL SURFACE: Metal surfaces, especially old ones, can rust and ruin your work, sometimes months or years after you have completed the project. For this reason, it is a good idea when working with a metal or tole object as a base for découpage to totally strip off old paint and/or varnish, apply a good rust remover, clean it with #0000 (superfine) steel wool, prime it with rust-resistant metal primer, paint, and start fresh. We are particularly fond, however, of old painted metal trays, and have on many occasions taken the risk of rust and worked right over the old paint. We cleaned the old surfaces with a little nonabrasive scouring powder, rinsed them with denatured alcohol, let the pieces dry thoroughly, glued our cutouts in place, and sealed it all with several coats of varnish. These pieces have continued to look beautiful over years of use. Since the work is built over the original old paint and detailing, they also retain their antique appearance.

PAINTING OR PAPERING A METAL SURFACE: Following the instructions for preparing a metal surface, you can totally strip and repaint a new or old metal piece for découpage. There are special paints made for use on metal, and others, like japan-base paints, will work on metal as well. If the process of stripping a metal piece and repainting it is more than you choose to do on your own, many antiques shops and furniture refinishers will do it for you. Certainly, as with wood, you can totally or partially paper a metal piece, using a good sizing and a strong adhesive.

WORKING ON A LAMINATE SURFACE: One of the most beautiful tables we photographed for this book, a blackground cocktail table with jungle flora and fauna, was, to our surprise, découpaged on a laminate top. Working on laminate has several advantages; these surfaces are perfectly smooth, offer even color, and require no real preparation other than a light sanding and dusting with a tack cloth. Apply cutouts with white craft glue and seal with varnish or polyurethane.

Choosing adhesives for découpage

Every découpeur has a favorite adhesive or two. The famous Hiram Manning created several of his very own, which he offered exclusively through the Hiram Manning Studio. Most are the more expected and widely available white or craft glues, Mod-Podge, and the like. In addition to these, we occasionally use vinyl or border adhesives, particularly when we are working with or over wallpapers or borders. You will have to decide which work best for you through practice and experimentation.

WHITE CRAFT GLUE: White craft glue, a polyvinyl chloride or polyvinyl acetate product, is traditionally recommended for découpage. Widely available under such trade names as Elmer's and Sobo, it can be used full strength or slightly diluted with water. It is nonstaining, water soluble until dry, and will not cause colors to bleed and fade. It sticks to wood, metal, glass, acrylic, plastic, laminate, and ceramic surfaces.

BORDER ADHESIVE: Border adhesive is good for applying borders or bits of wallpapers to small objects, either paper-on-paper or directly onto almost any surface. It adheres very quickly and is impossible to remove after it has dried. It is available at paint and paper stores.

PRIMER/ADHESIVE/SEALANT: This patented product, available under the trade name Mod Podge, is a water-base sealer, glue, and finish for all surfaces. It is available in matte and gloss finishes. Mod Podge must be thoroughly coated with a clear acrylic sealant after it has dried, to eliminate tackiness. Once it has dried, Mod Podge cannot be removed. It is available at art and craft supply stores.

GEL MEDIUM: A heavy-bodied, transparent gloss medium, this is an excellent art adhesive for collages. It will hold papers of all types, including cardboard, is water soluble, and will not become brittle when dry. It dries with a slight gloss. Designed for work that will not be extensively handled, it is available at art supply stores.

VINYL ADHESIVE: We use professional-strength clear vinyl adhesive for some découpage projects, particularly where a final coat of sealant is not necessary, such as picture mats, hatboxes, and lampshades. It works particularly well with lightweight papers, such as gift-wraps. Vinyl adhesive will not stick, however, on shiny paper surfaces. Since it is slower to dry than border adhesive, it allows you to move work around while you fine-tune the design. When dry, any excess will flake off and can be brushed away with a soft-bristle brush. Vinyl adhesive is available at paint and paper stores.

REMOVABLE-REUSABLE ADHESIVE: This putty-like material is nonoily and non-staining and can be used to temporarily hold cut pieces on a surface in order to position them before permanently applying them. Two brands widely available at art and craft supply stores are Plasti-Tak and E-Z-Tak.

Applying the elements

Like applying wallpaper, the aim of applying cutouts for découpage is to secure the paper on the base surface neatly and efficiently, with a minimum of handling and mess. The following are guidelines for the application of cutouts to a surface to create découpage:

APPLYING ADHESIVE: Most découpeurs suggest the use of slightly thinned white/craft glue applied to the backs of cutouts. (The exception is cutouts applied under glass, for which glue is applied to the face.) Others recommend applying the adhesive directly to the surface to be découpaged. In our experience, gluing the backs of the cutouts allows the adhesive to be absorbed quickly and effectively, is easier to control, and facilitates cleanup. In most cases, the glue can be applied with the finger or a small flat brush; for tiny, delicate gluing, a toothpick makes a good applicator. The amount of adhesive you apply is determined by the porosity of the paper, a judgment made from experience. This, like so much of découpage, requires experimentation. Too little glue and the cutout will not stick; too much and the cutout may be damaged from excessive handling and cleanup.

APPLYING THE CUTOUT: After the glue has set slightly, place the cutout on the surface and lightly tap it down with your finger or a bit of damp sponge. Starting in the center, gently roll and press with your finger to push the excess glue to the edges of the cutting, flattening out the air bubbles as you work. Your fingers are best for most jobs, but you can use a smoother, a small wallpaper seam roller, a special rubber roller called a brayer, or any combination of these that does the job. When you are applying small or delicate pieces of cut paper, laying a piece of kitchen wax paper over the pieces will help to hold them in place while you smooth or roll over the work. It is important to note here that some papers, particularly gift-wraps, will bubble up and wrinkle slightly as they begin to dry. In most cases, these imperfections will disappear as the piece dries thoroughly. If you have applied the glue evenly across the entire surface, and you have carefully applied the cutout by pushing excess glue out from the center and attending to all air bubbles as you go, this bubbling and wrinkling is not of your doing and the work will normally dry flat. Keep in mind that the objective is to secure the cutout firmly, with all of the edges tight and flat over a thin, even coating of glue.

CLEANING THE SURFACE: After all the elements are glued in place and have set up a bit, clean every bit of glue off the surface, using a damp sponge that has been dipped into hot water or white vinegar and wrung out. Rinse the sponge frequently to keep it clean. Clean delicate interior areas with a cotton swab dipped in white vinegar. Never let the paper get really wet.

Wipe carefully away from the edges, never in from the edges since this will tend to lift them off the surface. If you have used vinegar in this process, finish cleaning with pure water.

REMOVING AND REUSING A CUTTING AFTER GLUING: Should you change your mind about the exact placement of a cutting after it has been applied to the surface, it's not too late to make changes. Sometimes adding another element to the design to help or adjust an awkward placement is all you need. Other times you may want to completely remove an element and move it elsewhere in the design. This is easier when the glue is still tacky, but is possible even after the glue has dried. Squeezing hot water from a sponge onto the area, thoroughly wet the cutting, letting it soak for a minute or two. Then gently lift it up from a corner with the tip of your scissors or tweezers. Gently wash all the glue from the cutting, place it upside down on a flat surface, and let it dry before regluing and re-placing it in your découpage design.

REPAIRING AFTER GLUING: Sometimes an air bubble escapes notice until after the glue has dried. You can slit the piece with a craft knife, insert a little glue in the opening with a toothpick, and press the edges down firmly until they meet, leaving an invisible nick. Another problem you may encounter is corners that lift during the drying process or during the removal of an adjacent cutting. Reglue them, using a toothpick to reach under and apply a little bit of adhesive.

Choosing sealants for découpage

There are many sealants that will effectively protect and finish-coat your découpage work. Some require more fastidious effort than others; you must evaluate the seriousness of your project as well as the materials you used to make it, and then decide which coating in which degree of gloss finish to use. It is imperative that we mention here the issue of new and expanding environmental controls in the paint/sealant industry. At the time of the writing of this book, three states—New York, New Jersey, and California—have enacted legislation that restricts the sale of solvent-base paints and sealants because of their ecologically hazardous chemical components. It would be shortsighted to ignore what is certainly the beginning of a national, if not worldwide, trend. The impact of this developing awareness and related legislation strongly affects traditional découpage finishing techniques, which rely upon products that in some states are no longer available and, to the emerging national conscience, are no longer ecologically acceptable. Clearly, nonsolvent-base sealants offer easier and quicker finishing for découpage projects; it is for environmental reasons, however, that techniques incorporating water-base sealants are now most desirable. We include in our list traditional solvent-base products because it would be a grievous oversight to exclude them and their application from this book. We anticipate a developing technology in which ecologically safe sealants will offer the same level of artistic excellence.

VARNISH: The traditional découpage sealant of choice, varnishes such as McCloskey's famous "Heirloom," are solvent based, slow drying, and, therefore, smooth flowing and controllable. Varnishes are produced in a variety of finishes ranging from high gloss to low luster. High-gloss varnish is preferred for découpage because of its superior hardness and nonyellowing clarity. Traditionally, it is sanded to a soft sheen and may be further dulled by the addition of several coats of a low-luster varnish before waxing. Low-luster varnish has had flatting agents added to reduce sheen. When using low-luster varnish, it is essential to stir, not shake, the mixture in order to integrate the flatting agents into the varnish without causing air bubbles. (Varnish should never be shaken since the resulting bubbles are impossible to remove and will prevent successful application.) Most varnishes tend to yellow slightly, particularly with multiple coats, and will therefore change the colors of your work. Varnish does not keep well and should be purchased in small quantities to minimize waste. Varnish requires low humidity to dry successfully. Clean up with mineral spirits or paint thinner.

LACQUER: Unlike varnish, lacquer will dry extremely fast in high humidity, but it is far more likely to deteriorate and leaves a softer, more easily damaged finish. Lacquer cannot be successfully applied over shellac, varnish, or many paints. Lacquer is a tricky sealant for découpage, reacting negatively to the glue over a period of time. Flat black paint is the ideal background for découpage work you intend to seal with lacquer. Clean up with lacquer thinner.

SHELLAC: Shellac is a soft clear or amber wood finish prepared from "lac," a resinous substance produced by the banyan tree, dissolved in alcohol. Since a shellac finish will mar easily from water or alcohol, it is better used for work that will not be handled, such as découpage or collage intended to be hung on the wall. Shellac is not compatible with varnish; never use them together. Shellac can cause some dyes or paints to run. As with all sealant products, it is always wise to test it on a piece of scrap. Clean up with denatured alcohol.

POLYURETHANE: Polyvinylacetate varnishes, solvent based, quick drying, and thick, are excellent for the rapid buildup of heavy coats. Since they dry quickly, polyurethanes are difficult to control and cannot be easily brushed out to smooth the finish; they can, therefore, leave visible brush marks on the surface. They are available in a variety of finishes from high gloss to low luster. Like varnish, solvent-base polyurethanes tend to yellow, particularly when applied in multiple coats. Clean up with mineral spirits or paint thinner.

LATEX URETHANE: A water-soluble polyvinylacetate sealant (also sold under the name of latex urethane acrylic), this finish appears milky white in the can but dries "water clear." Like solvent-base polyurethanes, latex urethane comes in high-gloss to low-luster finishes,

dries quickly, and can be applied in thick coats. For the best application and smoothest finish, it should be applied with a well-flagged synthetic-bristle brush. Suitable for any surface, particularly where discoloration would be a problem, this sealant dries so perfectly clear that it is the best choice over white and pastel colors. Clean up with water.

MATTE MEDIUM: This water-soluble artist's mixing and glazing medium can be combined with an acrylic gloss medium to produce varying degrees of gloss. It is used as a glue in collage work and as a single-coat varnish finish; multiple coats will turn cloudy. Matte medium is best used on pieces to be placed under glass or in frames. Clean up with water.

PRIMER/ADHESIVE/SEALANT: This patented product, available under the trade name Mod Podge (as discussed on page 207 in "Choosing Adhesives for Découpage"), is a water-base sealer, glue, and finish in one. Available in matte and gloss finishes, Mod Podge must be thoroughly sealed with a clear acrylic after it has dried, to eliminate tackiness. Clean up with water.

Sealing découpage

The traditional methods for sealing découpage involve the application of a *minimum* of 20 coats of varnish. The process is further complicated by the need to sand between coats and to avoid working on rainy days. Should you wish to seal your projects in this traditional way, we describe the process for you. Few of the projects made for this book, however, involved more than 3 coats of polyurethane. The rule of thumb is to apply enough sealant to effectively sink the découpaged papers beneath a hard, smooth surface. To this end, many less demanding techniques will do the job.

TRADITIONAL SEALING: After the découpage is perfectly glued down, cleaned off, and dry, you can begin to apply varnish. Apply a generous coat of gloss varnish, using a soft flat ½-inch-wide brush for small objects, and up to a 2-inch brush for large projects like screens and tables. Apply at least 10 coats of gloss varnish, allowing at least 24 hours drying time between coats, totally sinking all the glued paper elements, covering all sides of the project equally, and checking all corners for drips. Do not varnish on a rainy day unless you are in an air-conditioned room. Use a tack cloth to dust the piece between coats. After the piece is totally dry, sand the work using 400-grit wet-and-dry sandpaper, dipped into water. There is a strong difference of opinion among traditional experts regarding the direction in which one should sand. Some suggest sanding with the grain; others

in overlapping circular motions. Whichever you choose, make sure the surface is sanded smooth with no pits or bumps and then wash it with water and dry it thoroughly. Apply approximately 10 more coats of varnish, depending upon the richness of the finish and the coloring you desire. The more coats of varnish, the more amber the tone of the piece. After the last coat is completely dry, sand smooth as before with 400-grit wet-and-dry sandpaper. This final sanding should give you a perfectly level, perfectly smooth surface. Clean the piece as described above, and wipe with a tack cloth before applying a final 2 coats of low-luster varnish. Then gently polish the surface with #0000 (superfine) steel wool to remove the tiny scratches from the sanding and all residual particles of steel wool. This is really the quickest of the traditional methods; some require twice as many steps. The master of the traditional method, Hiram Manning, for example, suggests a minimum of 20 coats of varnish before beginning to sand. Again, we suggest that you refer to one of the fine reference books on découpage to study these techniques in more detail.

QUICK SEALING: The objective of this simplified technique is basically the same as that of the more traditional process: to build up enough coats of sealant to totally sink the découpaged papers beneath a hard, smooth protective surface. To that end, polyurethane, either solvent based or latex, applied in several successive coats over the tightly glued cut work will effectively and quickly do the job. It will not, however, duplicate the exquisite finish of 20 or more coats of varnish, flowed over the surface, feathered out to obliterate all brush marks, patiently dried, and sanded and buffed to a satin patina. Polyurethane, unlike varnish, is designed to build up depth quickly and dry rapidly; both of these appealing properties make it impossible to control to the same degree that one can control the slower-drying, more forgiving varnish. In a very real sense, therefore, what you gain in speed and ease, you lose in refinement. Great care should be taken to apply polyurethanes as smoothly as possible, since brush marks will set up too quickly to feather. Sanding between coats, of course, will help this problem, and will enhance the piece's overall appearance. In general, four to five hours drying time should be adequate between coats, and four to six coats should be enough to sink the paper elements. Read the labels carefully, following suggested sanding procedures and drying times. One clear advantage of using polyurethane sealants is that they will provide superior protection against alcohol and water spotting and good resistance to abrasion. Another is purely health related. Unlike solvent-base sealants, latex urethane products are low-odor and nontoxic, noncombustible, and, in general, safer to use.

WAXING: When the last coat of sealant is perfectly dry, you may choose to wax the piece, using a damp cloth and a fine furniture paste or beeswax. We use commercially available Goddard's English paste wax and a soft French product called Mrs. Hudson's Fine Beeswax Polish, which is available through antiques stores in our area. In either case, the paste is applied sparingly with a cloth that has been thoroughly wet in cold water and then squeezed out. Pick up a little wax on the damp cloth and apply it over a small area, rubbing in a brisk circular motion. Add more wax as needed, being sure to keep your cloth damp, but don't over-apply the wax. Buff briskly to polish the piece, working quickly with a soft, lintless cloth. You may need to repeat this process until the surface finish is even. Pieces that have been waxed cannot have additional layers of sealant added at a later time without being meticulously cleaned and sanded down. Waxing adds patina to a piece, giving it a soft, warm glow.

Directory of Resources

What follows is a listing by category of the retail and wholesale firms, retail stores, manufacturers, mechanics, artists, craftspersons, and suppliers whose products and services are featured in this book. Please remember, however, that even though a particular wallpaper, border, art or handmade paper, gift-wrap, tool or craft material, supply, service, furnishing, antique, or accessory was available at the time we wrote this book, it may not be at the time you read it.

WALLPAPERS AND BORDERS MANUFACTURERS AND DISTRIBUTORS

**BOUSSAC
OF FRANCE, INC.**
979 Third Avenue
New York, NY 10022
(212) 421-0534
Through architects and
interior designers
Pages 2, 3, 33, 57, 86, 92,
104, 115

BRUNSCHWIG & FILS
979 Third Avenue
New York, NY 10022
(212) 838-7878
Through architects and
interior designers
Front jacket and pages 16,
26, 27, 28, 29, 34, 35, 38, 39,
40, 43, 48, 50, 53, 55, 58, 60,
61, 62, 63, 74, 76, 77, 78, 79,
83, 84, 85, 117, 123, 143,
151, 163, 166, 192, 200

CARLETON V LTD.
979 Third Avenue
New York, NY 10022
(212) 355-4525
Through architects and
interior designers
Pages 55, 78, 80, 81, 101

CAROLYN RAY, INC.
578 Nepperhan Avenue
Yonkers, NY 10701
(914) 476-0619
Through architects and
interior designers
Page 112

**CHARLES R. GRACIE
& SONS**
979 Third Avenue
New York, NY 10022
(212) 753-5350
Through architects and
interior designers
Pages 31, 70, 95

**CHRISTOPHER
HYLAND, INC.**
979 Third Avenue
New York, NY 10022
(212) 688-6121
Through architects and
interior designers
Pages 4, 5, 126, 194, 195

CLARENCE HOUSE
979 Third Avenue
New York, NY 10022
(212) 752-2890
Through architects and
interior designers
Front jacket, case covering,
and pages 14, 16, 20, 21, 28,
29, 53, 54, 68, 69, 74, 76, 77,
80, 81, 82, 101, 118, 173,
190, 191

COWTAN & TOUT, INC.
979 Third Avenue
New York, NY 10022
(212) 753-4488
Through architects and
interior designers
Endpapers and pages 25, 40,
52, 53, 67, 120, 161, 163

FONTHILL, LTD.
979 Third Avenue
New York, NY 10022
(212) 755-6700
Through architects and
interior designers
Front jacket and pages 2, 28,
29, 142, 151

HINES & CO.
979 Third Avenue
New York, NY 10022
(212) 685-8590
Through architects and
interior designers
half title

**NORTON BLUMENTHAL,
INC.**
979 Third Avenue
New York, NY 10022
(212) 752-2535
Through architects and
interior designers
Pages 30, 31, 34, 35, 50, 51,
70, 101

OSBORNE & LITTLE
979 Third Avenue
New York, NY 10022
(212) 751-3333
Through architects and
interior designers
Pages 22, 49, 50, 51, 52, 56,
71, 75, 77, 83, 95, 101, 103,
113, 177

ROGER ARLINGTON, INC.
979 Third Avenue
New York, NY 10022
(212) 752-5288
Through architects and
interior designers
Page 111

**SCALAMANDRE
SILKS, INC.**
950 Third Avenue
New York, NY 10022
(212) 980-3888
Through architects and
interior designers
Pages 72, 73, 96, 166, 167

SCHUMACHER
79 Madison Avenue
New York, NY 10016
(800) 552-9255
Through architects and
interior designers
Pages 67, 93, 105, 107, 113,
149, 157, 198, 199

STROHEIM & ROMANN
31-11 Thomson Avenue
Long Island City, NY 11101
(718) 706-7000
Through architects and
interior designers

THE TWIGS, INC.
5700 Third Street
San Francisco, CA 94124
(415) 822-1626
Through architects and
interior designers
Pages 48, 50, 51, 52, 70, 71,
74

WAVERLY
79 Madison Avenue
New York, NY 10016
(800) 423-5881
Through architects and
interior designers and select
retail stores
Pages 58, 62, 157

ZUBER & CIE
979 Third Avenue
New York, NY 10022
(212) 486-9226
Through architects and
interior designers
Page 87

RETAIL WALLPAPER STORES

JANOVIC PLAZA, INC.
1150 Third Avenue
New York, NY 10021
(212) 772-1400
Retail stores

WALLPAPER COTTAGE
76 Main Street
Chatham, NJ 07928
(201) 635-2021
Retail store

ANTIQUE AND COLLECTIBLE WALLPAPERS AND BORDERS

SECONDHAND ROSE
270 Lafayette Street
New York, NY 10012
(212) 431-7673
Retail store
Pages 12, 142, 164

SPECIAL TREATMENTS FOR PAPERS

TEX-RE-PEL, INC.
184 Broadway
Brooklyn, NY 11211
(718) 486-6502
Retail service

GIFT CARDS, STICKERS, AND GIFT-WRAPS

CASPARI GREETING CARDS
41 Madison Avenue
New York, NY 10021
(212) 685-9726
Through retail stores
Pages 66, 160

THE GIFTED LINE JOHN GROSSMAN, INC.
2656 Bridgeway
Sausalito, CA 94965-2429
(800) 5-GIFTED
(415) 332-4488
Through retail stores
Pages 125, 161, 164

THE WINSLOW PAPERS, INC.
231 Lawrenceville Road
Lawrenceville, NJ 08648
(609) 392-1333
Through retail stores
Pages 152, 161

HANDMADE AND ART PAPERS

ADVENTURES IN CRAFTS STUDIO
PO Box 6058
Yorkville Station
New York, NY 10128
(212) 410-9793
Découpage supplies and
elements by mail order

AIKO'S ART MATERIALS IMPORT
3347 North Clark Street
Chicago, IL 60657
(312) 404-5600
Retail store and mail order
Page 142

KATE'S PAPERIE
8 West 13th Street
New York, NY 10011
(212) 633-0570
Retail store
Page 15

**NEW YORK CENTRAL ART
SUPPLY INC.**
62 Third Avenue
New York, NY 10003
(212) 473-7705
Retail store

PEARL PAINT CO.
308 Canal Street
New York, NY 10013
(800) 221-6845
(212) 431-7932
Retail store
Pages 68, 69, 100

ARTISTS AND
CRAFTSPERSONS

ANYA LARKIN
39 West 28th Street
New York, NY 10001
(212) 532-3263
Through architects and
interior designers
Pages 15, 17

**CHARLES PUZZO
SPECIALTY WALLS**
Through Donna Lang LTD
180 Main Street
Chatham, NJ 07928
(201) 635-4805
Painter/wallpaperer
Pages 13, 27, 34, 35, 49, 52,
53, 57, 58, 61, 62, 64, 65, 67,
68, 69, 71, 74, 75, 76, 77, 78,
79, 118, 163

**DAVID MADISON
HORTICULTURAL DESIGN
(DMHD)**
251 East 62nd Street
New York, NY 10021
(212) 421-8110
Retail store
Pages 31, 33, 49, 52, 53, 57,
87, 101, 145

**DECORATOR'S
WORKSHOP**
504 East 74th Street
New York, NY 10021
Drapery/upholstery
workroom
(212) 879-6559
Pages 38, 49, 87

HIRAM MANNING
Boston, MA 02120
Découpage artist
Pages 15, 16, 106

**HOLSTEN INTERIOR
ARTISANS**
196 Grove Street
Ramsey, NJ 07446
(201) 327-6614
Paper and faux-finish artist
Page 23

JERED HOLMES
404 East 55th Street
New York, NY 10022
(212) 935-0885
Découpage artist
Pages 17, 109, 154, 169

**JUDITH A. PETERSEN
ENTERPRISES**
19 Sherman Avenue
Summit, NJ 07901
(908) 277-3994
Drapery/accessory
workroom
Front jacket and pages 28,
29, 49, 62, 67, 71, 74, 163

JUDITH STRAETEN
205 West 89th Street
New York, NY 10024
(212) 838-7878
(212) 595-5740
Découpage artist
Page 143

MARY P. HAVLICEK
Fanwood, NJ 07023
Découpage artist
Pages 108, 172

NICOLA WINGATE SAUL
47 Moreton Terrace
London SW1 V2NS
England
·Print-room artist
Pages 46, 47

RALPH CAPARULO
122 Montclair Avenue
Montclair, NJ 07042
(201) 783-4736
Artist
Pages 92, 102, 129

STESSL & NEUGEBAUER
9 Industrial Place
Summit, NJ 07901
(908) 277-3340
Drapery/upholstery
workroom
Through architects and
interior designers
Pages 68, 69

VINCENT LAVECCHIA
928 Park Avenue
Elizabeth, NJ 07208
(908) 527-6109
Cover photograph and
pages 28, 29, 72

ANTIQUES, COLLECTIBLES, AND ACCESSORIES

AGOSTINO ANTIQUES, LTD.
808 Broadway
New York, NY 10003
(212) 533-5566
Retail store
Page 150

CIRCA DAVID BARRETT, LTD.
323 East 59th Street
New York, NY 10022
(212) 688-0950
Through architects and interior designers
Page 49

DAVID DUNCAN ANTIQUES
227 East 60th Street
New York, NY 10022
(212) 688-0666
Retail store
Page 23

IVORY BIRD ANTIQUES
555 Bloomfield Avenue
Montclair, NJ 07042
(201) 746-6223
Retail store
Pages 97, 139, 161

JOHN ROSSELLI INTERNATIONAL CORP.
523 East 73rd Street
New York, NY 10021
(212) 772-2137
Through architects and interior designers
Pages 90, 112, 131

LIMITED EDITIONS
253 East 72nd Street
New York, NY 10021
(212) 249-5563
Retail store
Pages 119, 148

NEWEL ART GALLERIES, INC.
425 East 53rd Street
New York, NY 10022
(212) 758-1970
Retail store
Pages 81, 87, 145

NICHOLAS ANTIQUES
979 Third Avenue
New York, NY 10022
(212) 688-3312
Retail store
Pages 35, 52, 57

FURNITURE AND ACCESSORIES

IKEA, U.S., INC.
Plymouth Meeting, PA 19462
(215) 834-0180
Retail stores
Pages 144, 146, 147

JAMES H. HARRIS & CO., INC.
2 Mill Street
Cornwall, NY 12518
(914) 534-3850
Through architects and interior designers
Page 52

LYLE & UMBACH, LTD.
15 Cosdrew Lane
East Hampton, NY 11937
(516) 324-3830
Pages 49, 87

SUMMIT GLASS SHOWCASE
465 Springfield Avenue
Summit, NJ 07901
(908) 277-0365
Retail store
Pages 49, 75, 79, 80, 81

LAMPS AND LIGHTING SUPPLIES

ANNE FILKIN LAMPS & SHADES
328 Bloomfield Avenue
Caldwell, NJ 07006
(201) 228-9038
Retail store
Page 123

ORIENTAL LAMP SHADE CO., INC.
816 Lexington Avenue
New York, NY 10021
(212) 832-8190
Retail store
Page 124

WILLIAMS LAMPS
765 Central Avenue
Westfield, NJ 07090
(908) 232-2158
Retail store
Page 127

PRINTS AND FRAMED ART

ARGOSY BOOK STORE
116 East 59th Street
New York, NY 10022
(212) 753-4455
Retail store
Page 96

THE METROPOLITAN MUSEUM OF ART
1000 Fifth Avenue
New York, NY 10028
(800) 468-7386
Retail store
Front jacket and pages 102, 151

J. POCKER & SON, INC.
135 East 63rd Street
New York, NY 10021
(800) 443-3116
(212) 838-5488
Retail store
Pages 49, 50, 51, 52, 54, 100, 105, 107, 113, 170, 171, 206, 207, 212

URSUS PRINTS
981 Madison Avenue
New York, NY 10021
(212) 772-8787
Retail store
Pages 14, 150

INTERIOR DESIGNERS

ALBERT HADLEY PARISH HADLEY ASSOCIATES, INC.
305 East 63rd Street
New York, NY 10021
(212) 888-7979
Pages 141, 168

ANTHONY ANTINE, ISID ANTINE ASSOCIATES, INC.
1028 Arcadian Way
Palisades, NJ 07024
(201) 224-0315
Pages 96, 100, 108

BARBARA LAZARUS
10 Fones Alley
Providence, RI 02906
(401) 521-8910
Pages 25, 44

CAROLYN BRONSON CREATIVE WALLS BY BRONSON DESIGN STUDIO
207 Bellevue Avenue
Upper Montclair, NJ 07043
(201) 783-3611
Retail store
Page 126

GEORGIANA STOCKEL GEORGIANA STOCKEL INTERIOR DESIGN
80 South Mountain Avenue
Montclair, NJ 07042
(201) 744-5642
Page 126

LIBBY CAMERON PARISH HADLEY ASSOCIATES, INC.
305 East 63rd Street
New York, NY 10022
(212) 888-7979
Pages 39, 110, 119, 131

MAGGIE TAYLOR THE TAYLORS
608 Lawrence Avenue
Westfield, NJ 07090
(908) 654-6018
Pages 97, 127

MARK ALAN POLO, ISID, ALLIED ASID POLO, M.A.
1107 Buckingham Road
Fort Lee, NJ 07024
(201) 224-0322
Page 91

MELINDA JOHNSON, ASID BOXWOOD HOUSE, INC.
44 North Dean Street
Englewood, NJ 07631
(201) 871-3323
(201) 871-0667
Page 23

MICHAEL ZABRISKI MCMILLEN INC.
155 East 56th Street
New York, NY 10022
(212) 753-6377
Pages 89, 119

PATRICIA ROTH MICHAEL LOVE QUANTUM DESIGNS
121 Madison Avenue
New York, NY 10016
(212) 545-0301
Page 90

STUART SCHEPPS, ISID, ASID DSGN INTERIOR DESIGN INCORPORATED
181 Longhill Road
Little Falls, NJ 07424
(201) 785-4626
Page 102

Acknowledgments

We are awed by the lengthy list of friends, clients, manufacturers, interior designers, and artists/craftspersons who worked with us on this project. May this acknowledgment in some small way say thank-you to them all, including:

The ever-challenging and gifted Dennis Krukowski, who brings vision, artistic brilliance, and philosophy along with his magic Hasselblad; Pam Krauss, Pam Krauss, Pam Krauss (last time we ran through three editors—this time Pam had to be the entire trio)—multitalented, multifaceted, and our prime source of the best sushi in New York; Mrs. Henry Parish II for her support and validation of this project; Howard Klein, our art director, with his gentle authority and magnetic brown eyes; Karen Grant and Andrzej Janerka, book designers; Charlie Puzzo, our gifted and innovative painter/paperhanger who gives new meaning to the words "artistic," "cooperative," and "I'll be a little late"; Mary Havlicek, our dear friend and talented artist/craftsperson, with her tiny flashing scissors, specs, and smorgasbord of glue containers; David Madison, the Flower Man, who can be counted on for his outrageously beautiful bouquets and his outrageous charm; Hiram Manning, découpeur and raconteur extraordinaire, who entertained and educated us; the many manufacturers and distributors of papers whose courtesy and enthusiasm were integral to this effort, most especially Temo Callahan of Clarence House, who never refused a call or a request, Eric Kennedy at Osborne & Little, who kept placing orders for one roll of this or that without complaint and without thinking that we had finally lost our minds, Connie and Arthur Athas at The Twigs, for the caryatid papers that truly inspired the whole book, Michael Silverman and the crew at Boussac, who encouraged us to try out this concept three years ago in the showroom foyer, and Murray Douglas and her remarkable staff at Brunschwig, who were so supportive from the very beginning. Special thanks to all the clients and friends who opened their homes or shops to us, especially Joel and Susan Simon, Mrs. Bobbie Crosby, David and Joy Simon, Peter and Ruth Perretti, Norm and Judy Polonofsky, Gene and Janie Goodwillie, the Junior League of Montclair/Newark "Centennial" Designer Showhouse, Kate's Paperie, Secondhand Rose, John Rosselli, and Boussac of France; the talented and gracious designers who allowed us to photograph their work, especially Tony Antine of Antine Associates, Melinda Johnson of Boxwood House, Maggie Taylor of The Taylors, Stuart Schepps of DSGN Interiordesign, Carolyn Bronson and Georgiana Stockel, Mark Polo, Michael Zabriski of McMillen, Albert Hadley and Libby

Cameron of Parish Hadley, and Judy and Pete Petersen; and the extraordinary artists, artist/designers, and craftspersons whose work or individual pieces of découpage appear on these pages, especially Mrs. Henry Parish II and Diane Miller of Parish Hadley, Mrs. Apple Bartlett, Mrs. D.B. Gilbert, Mr. Hiram Manning, Ralph Caparulo, Anya Larkin, Liz Galbraith, Cal Ling, John Campbell, and the delightful Jered Holmes; Joseph Lang and Bill Robertson, who once again brought their love and support to this project; and our remarkable sons, Wes, Evan, Ian, and Keith, who have carried on brilliantly with the complicated business of growing up into responsible and successful young people and have given us more pleasure than we could ever find the words to say. We thank you, one and all.

Index